BUILDING THE CATHEDRAL

ANSWERING THE MEANING CRISIS
THROUGH PERSONAL MYTH

SADIE ALWYN MOON

VOLUME IV
METAMODERN SPIRITUALITY SERIES
Edited by Brendan Graham Dempsey

Palimpsest Press

Metamodern Spirituality Series
VOLUME IV
Building the Cathedral: Answering the Meaning Crisis through Personal Myth
Sadie Alwyn Moon

FROM THE EDITOR

Metamodernism is the cultural paradigm that has superseded postmodernism, and is visible all around us through the art and ideas now shaping the world. According to some, it is even more than that: a whole philosophical approach, and a developmental stage reached by individuals and entire cultures alike as they progress through higher and higher levels of complex thinking. In this view, society has gone from traditional thinking, to modern, postmodern, and, finally, metamodern thinking, advancing in depth and awareness along the way while continually integrating the crucial insights of all the previous stages that have gone before.

This series aims to address various spiritual topics and concerns that arise at this metamodern stage. As such, it is not for everyone. Metamodern spirituality is still in its nascent formations. Like a star being born in a nebula, things are still highly volatile, and highly dangerous. Like a star, what is emerging here may eventually come to seed the universe with life-giving celestial grandeur... or hypernova everything *to smithereens*. We are quite literally playing with god-stuff. Since the distribution of metamodern-stage thinking is thought to follow a normal distribution curve, the vast majority of the population is still traditional or modern in mindset (topped by a smattering of true postmodernists up in their ivory towers). For most, then, the texts in this series may be safely passed over as obtuse arcana. For some, though, they may come as mana from heaven. Ultimately, the goal is to help bridge the gap between: to help update the cultural code for *everyone*, however "flattened" the result (so long as the result doesn't flatten us!).

To engage so broad a potential readership certainly requires a broad array of authors. As it is, I am only one man. And so I hope I may at least be serviceable in this effort as a *general editor*—to bring together in one series a symphony of voices, all speaking to metamodern spirituality in their own way, on their own topics and with their own approaches. Here I am inspired by no less singular a metamodernist as

Hanzi Freinacht, the eminent sociologist and political philosopher and author of the *Metamodern Guide to Politics* series. As he notes, the new metamodern philosophical paradigm requires an even deeper perspectival approach than what modern or postmodern philosophical discourse has to offer. Sacred as the "single individual" is, we would be lying to ourselves if we failed to acknowledge sociology's insight that our psyche is an imprint of the collective world, or psychology's insight that a collective world comprises our psyche. We are, to quote Hanzi (quoting Deleuze), "dividuals," which is to say "full of different parts, of different voices and drives working in different contexts." For the whole truth to be spoken authoritatively, then, it must be spoken by different authors. One needs, that is, an A. Severan to address metamodernism from a postmodern standpoint, a Sadie Alwyn Moon to get at metamodern mythmaking from a traditional angle, etc. Else we leave the world in the dust (perhaps as Anti-Kierkegaard and Anti-Nietzsche threaten to do). Thus, what Hanzi says of irony is true of polyphony as well:

> the distance-creating irony and sarcasm are what allow me to be perfectly honest and genuine with you, to be absurdly sincere and thereby ridiculously vulnerable. …Without the irony and the sarcasm, my sincerity would simply be too much.

One seeks to be comprehensive (indeed, no one more so than a general editor). I am but a channel, then, for these different channels. As such, I am really rather little myself, no? So I humbly submit, anyway. I would not so boldly claim to rise to the level that a metamodern philosopher like Hanzi Freinacht seeks. If, "[t]o the dialectically inclined political philosopher, followers are made of bronze, informed critics of silver and spiritual adversaries of molten gold," what base metal is a mere editor? Lower than metal, perhaps, until I prove mine. Through ivory and horn I go a'shuffling, collating the Sibyl's lost leaves as best I can this side of Paradise.

Ah, but I fear false humility is its own form of baseness—its own pretense. If so, it's a mask I'd sooner wear over the blustering Übermensch philosopher, high up his Alps. May it work just as well. "In this ironic game, we can play with our identities, with who we are, who we want to become, what we seek to create, with reality itself and with what we must achieve." Indeed, to do metamodern philosophy (/theology?) demands no less.

Be that as it may, it matters little to me. Series aside, I have abandoned more serious endeavors—academia, for instance, or gathering Federal Reserve Notes into barns. I am free to play, then, as but an editor, untethered to the shackles now in vogue, and let the speakers in this series do the real work. Perhaps *they* are what the metamodern philosopher seeks, those "resourceful and imaginative co-creators." Such co-creators "recognize the tune I am playing," says Hanzi, "join in the dance, and playfully re-create society and reality." Such is the very task of metamodern spirituality, it would seem. But of that topic I'll let the series authors speak for themselves, the curtain now raised, with no more preemption from me than this play's prologue.

Brendan Graham Dempsey
The Ides of March 2021, Vermont

iii

PREFACE

Tolstoy wrote, "All happy families resemble one another; every unhappy family is unhappy in its own way." The same could be said about individuals' relationship to myth and meaning. Anyone with a working, living myth will feel rooted, whole, and meaningful in much the same way. By contrast, there are countless ways in which a person's relationship to myth might be broken or warped.

Perhaps they were raised in a myth they can no longer accept and so find themselves disillusioned. Perhaps they confuse their myth with history and literal fact. Perhaps they were never introduced to a mythic orientation at all—or were even taught to denigrate mythic orientations as inherently stupid and superstitious.

Subjective experience will vary accordingly. For one person, it might be a chronic background sense of unease and uncertainty; for another, depression. Some may bury their anxieties and try to simply distract themselves from the problem (with work, say, or intoxicants.). Others will frantically search for something— *anything*—to fill the hole, and turn to all sorts of quasi-mythic frameworks in desperation.

Today, unfortunately, such broken myths are proliferating all around us—in cults, conspiracy theories, fundamentalist religions and fanatical political ideologies. People are turning to these broken myths in hopes of resolving their own broken relationship to meaning in a culture with no collective myth. However, such makeshift substitutes for viable, living myths prove, without fail, to be destructive and, ultimately, unfulfilling. Nevertheless, these sorts of myth-substitutes will continue to spread and gain prominence until our cultural crisis finds some workable, long-term resolution.

As the last great cultural myth of Christianity continues to recede with no new collective myth taking its place, a vacuum has been opening. Some have called this widening abyss "the meaning crisis," and it will continue to swallow us up until some sustainable answer for our times is found. This book aims to propose a possible solution to this crisis. As such, it is addressed to that large and growing number of people who have no working, living relationship to myth. For those comfortably served by some religion or another, this book will offer very little. It is written instead for the seekers, the doubters, the individualists uncomfortable with creeds and dogmas and codes, and those looking to find their own way through the desert. It is written for the "nones," that growing demographic of religiously "non-affiliated" souls who may slink from Churches but still seek insight and assurances from their experience. It is for the "spiritual but not religious" folks, whose sense of sacredness exists outside the box, and will not be confined to what's been given. It is my belief that the New Myth is already living in such souls. It only remains to draw it out and build it up.

Sadie Alwyn Moon

TABLE OF CONTENTS

SURVEYING

HORIZONS

The renowned comparative mythologist Joseph Campbell once noted: "If you want to see what a society really believes in, look at what the biggest buildings on the horizon are dedicated to." Our horizons tell our stories; skylines speak.

In the 13th century, at the peak of medieval piety, the air was flooded with countless collective efforts: mighty, multi-generational enterprises, accreting slowly: communal prayers in stone—the great *cathedrals*—rising heavenward...

Today, our cities pronounce a different set of values. Sleek skyscrapers loom up from the financial districts of the world like obelisks of glass; stark office-buildings and luxury apartment-complexes cast their concrete shadows onto the streets below; and, touching the clouds, metallic monuments to global trade shimmer like crystal mirrors of the empty air.

Our horizons tell our stories; they are the silhouettes left by our myths—which is to say, our dreams, our aspirations, our great purposes. Campbell also noted: "The rise and fall of civilizations in the long, broad course of history can be seen to have been largely a function of the integrity and cogency of their supporting canons of myth; for not authority but *aspiration* is the motivator, builder, and transformer of civilization."[1]

The question then naturally arises: What is *our* aspiration?

What motivates us, today, in the 21st century? What is our purpose? What is our myth?

The *change* in horizons tells its own story. Like the horizon, it is big, and like all big stories, it is somewhat overtold—though no less true for that. Like a skyline, the story has many components, but one broad shape. So, whether you focus on this part or that—the scientific revolution, say, or industrialization, secularization, rationalism, statism, capitalism—the takeaway impression is still the same. From Saint-Denis to St. Regis, from Aachen to Aon, one reads in the difference a long, clear tale. It is a story of *disenchantment*—of losing the soaring magic and meaning of our lives to the banality of things: to commerce, comfort, and commodity.

And myth? *"In what myth does man live nowadays?"* Carl Jung, the pioneering psychologist, asked himself a decade into the 20th century. "In the Christian myth, the answer might be," he proposed from a Europe still nominally Christian. Though, "Christian Europe," even by Jung's time, was a mostly-spent force. The old moral God, whose myth of Adam's sin and Christ's redemption once held the Western world in thrall, was dead (as Nietzsche had recognized a generation earlier), even though His shadow would persist on the Earth for some time. No, the epoch of the old Christian religion was drawing to its close. And the Christian myth?

The introspective psychologist wrestled internally:

"Do you live in it?" I asked myself.
To be honest, the answer was no. For me, it is not what I live by.
"Then do we no longer have any myth?"
"No, evidently we no longer have any myth."
"But then what is *your* myth—the myth in which you *do* live?"
At this point the dialogue with myself became uncomfortable, and I stopped thinking. I had reached a dead end.[2]

What is your myth—the myth in which you do live...?

Human beings are mythic creatures. It is our myths that inspire our most meaningful and enduring actions. It is our myths that build and motivate our civilizations, that lead us to forge pyramids and cathedrals in communal efforts spanning centuries. So what does it mean for us today, when *myth itself* seems to have reached a dead end? What does it mean for each of us, individually, that our cultural myth is no longer living? From what are *you* to derive your sense of purpose, direction, and motivation?

What is your myth?

Jung was at a crisis point in his life when he realized the absence of myth in his life. It was, he would later write in his memoir *Memories, Dreams, Reflections,*[3] a "period of inner uncertainty" and "disorientation," a time during which he felt "suspended in mid-air," without a clear footing or foundation for his existence. In this state of crisis, writes Jung,

> I was driven to ask myself in all seriousness: "What is the myth you are living?"
> I found no answer to this question, and had to admit that I was not living with a myth, or even in a myth, but rather in an uncertain cloud of theoretical possibilities which I was beginning to regard with increasing distrust...
> So, in the most natural way, I took it upon myself to get to know "my" myth, and I regarded this as the task of tasks...[4]

In 1912, the psychologist's psychic turmoil had begun to manifest in a series of strange dreams. Bizarre images rattled his unconscious—experiences similar, he knew, to those recounted by the psychotic patients he treated at the asylum where he had worked. Jung was concerned. But, rather than run from the problem, the intrepid psychoanalyst committed himself to confronting the issue head-on. After all, how could he expect his patients to work through their psychic disturbances if their own doctor couldn't work through his? Seeing no other way, all he could do was give in to his intuition and let instinct guide him to some resolution. "I consciously submitted myself," he says, "to the impulses of the unconscious."[5] Finding no living myth for himself in the spiritual desert which modern, secular society had become, Jung turned to the last font that still seemed to flow with any vital energies: *his own inner world*—his experience, his dreams, his fantasies, the pressing material of his own unconscious.

When he did, a flash of inspiration eventually struck. A childhood memory rose: a memory of... playing...

... building with blocks...

Simple though it was, the memory stirred him. Amidst a spiritual desert, Jung felt he had struck a spring of still-living water within himself. "There is still life in these things," he marveled. "The small boy is still around, and possesses a creative life which I lack."[6] True to his purpose, Jung gave himself over to the impulse—to see what it might yield.

The 37-year-old doctor began *to play*.

I started building: cottages, a castle, a whole village. The church was still missing, so I made a square building with a hexagonal drum on top of it, and a dome. A church also requires an altar, but I hesitated to build that. Preoccupied with the question of how I could approach this task, I was walking along the lake as usual one day, picking up stones out of the gravel on the shore. Suddenly I caught sight of a red

4

stone, a four-sided pyramid about an inch and a half high. It was a fragment of stone which had been polished into this shape by the action of the water—a pure product of chance. I knew at once: this was the altar![7]

Jung let himself become lost in play, tapping into his inner creative child, *building cathedrals...*

Of course, being a scientist, he was also well aware what an odd figure he now struck—a grown man playing with stones. His conscious, critical perspective loudly resisted. "Naturally," he writes,

> I thought about the significance of what I was doing, and asked myself, "Now, really, what are you about? You are building a small town, and doing it as if it were a rite!" I had no answer to my question, only the inner certainty that I was on the way to discovering my own myth.[8]

Jung refused to let critical self-awareness stop him. About his play, he was quite serious. The dignified psychologist kept playing with his rocks on the beach.

And, indeed, his little game of enchantment paid off. "In the course of this activity," he writes, "my thought clarified, and I was able to grasp the fantasies whose presence in myself I dimly felt."[9] His "building game," it turned out, was "only a beginning." It now unleashed a torrent of dreams and images from his unconscious. Play had broken the dam, and the spring became a river. So, like before with his stones, Jung channeled it into *construction* and *creativity.*

Transcribing the content of his new mental visions onto the pages of a large red folio journal, Jung would paint his symbolic dreams in vivid color, with an accompanying script of intricate calligraphy worthy of the finest illuminated manuscripts. Fantastic scenes, and even distinct unconscious personas—such as a wise guide-figure named Philemon, whom he hauntingly depicted flying aloft on kingfisher's wings—now populated the pages of a strange, personal scripture: Jung's *Red Book*, inspired by his unconscious.

(Pages from Jung's *Red Book*)

Such symbolic figures were representative of "the fund of unconscious images which fatally confuse the mental patient," Jung knew. "But it is also the matrix of a mythopoeic [mythmaking] imagination which had vanished from our rational age."[10] The process of reconnecting with this matrix was precisely what Jung needed to explore *his myth*.

As before, he persisted with his constructive project even as his rational mind retained a critical awareness that cast doubt on his enterprise. "When I was writing down these fantasies," he remembers,

> I once asked myself, "What am I really doing? Certainly this has nothing to do with science. But then what is it?" Whereupon a voice within me said, "It is art." I was astonished. It had never entered my head that what I was writing had any connection with art.[11]

Though Jung had not set out to produce art, and would later give up the *Red Book* for a more analytical approach to his visions, he would never leave behind *creative construction* as a means of exploring and articulating his myth. Indeed, such expression, he ultimately recognized, *was* his myth. Finding some way to make conscious and material the images formerly hidden and invisible in the unconscious was itself his life's mission, his personal myth. As he says succinctly in the very first sentence of his memoir, "My life is a story of the self-realization of the unconscious." It is ultimately to that end that he labored. That was the story and the meaning of his life.

Once hit upon, Jung expressed that myth in all he did, from the *Red Book*, to his scientific writings, to his own autobiography. As it turned out, though, his true medium of choice was not in these, but already hinted at earlier, in that initial spark of intuition which first broke open his unconscious for exploration:

Building.

Playing with stones had put Jung back in touch with his mythopoeic imagination; eventually, he would hew his very myth through them. "Gradually," he writes,

7

through my scientific work, I was able to put my fantasies and the contents of the unconscious on a solid footing. Words and paper, however, did not seem real enough to me; something more was needed. I had to achieve a kind of representation in stone of my innermost thoughts and of the knowledge I had acquired. Or, to put it another way, I had to make a confession of faith in stone. That was the beginning of the "Tower," the house which I built for myself at Bollingen.[12]

For the remainder of his life, Jung worked the stones at Bollingen into a mighty structure that contained, in architectural form, the very essence of his person. "From the beginning," he writes, "I felt the Tower as in some way a place of maturation—a maternal womb or a maternal figure in which I could become what I was, what I am and will be. It gave me the feeling as if I were being reborn in stone."[13] From the symbolic reliefs Jung carved into its walls, to the schematic layout that finally materialized ("only afterward did I see how all the parts fitted together"),[14] Jung labored to present his personal myth in monumental rock.

Horizons tell our stories; skylines speak. At Bollingen, a novel structure rose into the air: Jung's Tower, telling his. At the building's core, the Swiss psychologist built a private chapel—a quiet meditation room, to which he alone kept the key. (The land, after all, had originally been owned by a nearby monastery...)

Jung was building *his cathedral*.

Hewn from the raw material of his own experience, this was one man's temple, a shrine to the God he had discovered—and dedicated his life to continue discovering—within *himself*.

What does it mean to work on something like that? What does it mean to give yourself to a project that demands your complete commitment, that incorporates and valorizes the totality of who you are? The builders of the 13th century aspired to a God above; what about cathedrals to the God *within*? What role might *they* play in a world otherwise given over to the smallness of material and mundane things—to the daily grind of getting and spending?

What could our horizons look like?

An individual is unique, true; but some can be *exemplary*. Finding your own way can help lead others to theirs. For all his emphasis on "individuation"—that demanding task of carving for yourself in the world, and learning to express your *own* individual vision—Jung never sought monastic renunciation or turned his back on the world. Indeed, it was largely the prospect of being able to help his patients by means of his experience that drove him to gaining wisdom of the unconscious. He was, first and foremost, a psychiatrist: a "doctor of the soul." His life's work was his medicine. Today, Jung's methods are employed around the world; his writings have become the seminal canon for a whole field, to which new generations are continually adding. In this way, Jung's Tower is itself only part of a much larger cathedral, one that is still being built and developed through a vast communal effort.

After a long and arduous psychological process, Carl Jung eventually found the answers he was looking for. Individually, *on his own*, he had succeeded in re-centering himself in myth and finding true purpose in the work of a lifetime. By looking beyond his culture's depleted religious system and developing his own personal myth, Jung had found a way back to the vital source, to the unified unconscious Self, to what the religions call "God"—and one that led directly through *his own biography*. This labor activated a community, and continues to provide tools for personal growth even today.

Now, almost a hundred years later, Jung's "task of tasks" has become ours—and one more urgent and necessary than ever. The last collective myth has receded even further; the shadow of God grows dim; and, in the sky, our Earth's horizons darken with ever-taller metropolitan monoliths to Money: the only generally-recognized worth in a world shorn of higher purposes. If we are to find true meaning and fulfilment, there is no longer any choice now but to look *within*, as Jung did—not just for ourselves, but for the world. And, as for him, the way lies through the development of your *personal myth.*

PERSONAL MYTH

So, what exactly is personal myth? In the decades since Jung first introduced it, the term has gone on to acquire a somewhat diffuse array of meanings as subsequent generations of psychologists and mythologists have developed the idea in slightly different directions. Nevertheless, in spite of this diversity, there are a number of key elements about which all more or less agree.

Among these consensus points is the *impetus* for personal myth: namely, the growing inability of cultural myth (i.e., traditional religions) to provide people a sense of meaning, and the transference of that responsibility to the individual. As Stephen Larsen, one of Joseph Campbell's protégées and author of *The Mythic Imagination: The Quest for Meaning Through Personal Mythology*, puts it: "Mythology was, perforce, collective mythology. But in our modern times these forms have relaxed their collective grip on the psyche, placing the burden for a meaningful experience of the universe on the individual person."[15] Indeed, as Campbell himself wrote, "[W]e can no longer look to communities for the generation of myth. *The mythogenetic zone today is the individual in contact with his own interior life...*"[16] Some form of this sentiment is shared by virtually all writers on personal myth.

This idea leads directly to another universally-recognized feature of personal myth: Because the locus of myth and mythmaking has shifted from the inherited cultural tradition to the individual's inner life, it is in our own *experience* that we must seek the inspiration and material from which to craft our myth. So, as Dan McAdams says in *The Stories We Live By: Personal Myths and the Making of the Self*, "The personal myth is... a sacred story that embodies personal truth. To say that a personal myth is 'sacred' is to suggest that a personal myth deals with those ultimate questions that preoccupy theologians and philosophers."[17] The traditional idea of "sacred history" is thus converted to something like "sacred biography." Meaning is found not through participation in a group's relation to the divine (e.g., the Church, the people of Israel, etc.), but in seeing your *own* story as meaningful, in forging your *own* link to the sacred.

At a basic level, then, a personal myth can be understood as *an individual's narrative of meaning, developed out of their own experience, which fulfills for them what cultural myths once provided but no longer can.* In their book *Personal Mythology*, David Feinstein and Stanley Krippner write:

> Personal myths speak to the broad concerns of identity (Who am I?), direction (Where am I going?), and purpose (Why am I going there?). For an internal system of images, narratives, and emotions to be called a personal myth, it must address at least one of the core concerns of human existence, the traditional domains of cultural mythology.[18]

11

If personal myths effectively operate as individual substitutes for cultural myths, we will need to understand what functions cultural myths used to perform if we are to see how these might be effectively transferred to the sphere of the individual. Here Feinstein and Krippner rightly direct us to Joseph Campbell's oft-cited "four functions of mythology" for guidance.

According to Campbell, myths fulfill what he calls a psychological, metaphysical, cosmological, and a sociological function:

> Myth's **psychological function** is to center the individual, carry them through the stages of development, and harmonize them with their world.

> Myth's **metaphysical function** is to awaken in the individual a sense of awe and gratitude for the ultimate mystery, reconciling them to reality as it is.

> Myth's **cosmological function** is to present a total image of the universe through which the ultimate mystery manifests.

> Myth's **sociological function** is to validate and maintain a certain moral order of laws for living with others in society. [19]

In premodern/traditional societies, the inherited cultural myth-systems functioned (more or less) successfully on *all* of the levels, providing individuals guidance through 1) their life's developmental crises and transformations, 2) a framework for relating themselves to the Ultimate Mystery, 3) an explanatory orientation for meaningfully navigating their world, and 4) a sense of how to treat other individuals in their community. When all of these needs are met and harmoniously integrated, the individual will feel in alignment with herself and her world: a state experienced as a sense of *meaning* and *wholeness.*

As noted, however, the transformation of our horizons has reconfigured society along entirely different lines from the old premodern, mythic ones—a process completed in the 20ᵗʰ century, though set in motion much earlier.* As of yet, no one has found a means to put the pieces back together in our new world— that is, to re-integrate a meaningful mythic existence with the developments of modern life. I believe that *personal myth offers us a path to do just this.*

However, it will require us to see the bigger picture. To date, no writers on the topic have been so bold in their suggestions as I would like to be. Most tend to speak as though personal myth were just another form of therapy, its impacts confined entirely to a patient's psyche. Recall, for instance, how Feinstein and Krippner suggest that a personal myth, if it is to warrant the title, must address "at least one" of Campbell's four functions. But why so *few?* Why can't personal mythmaking address *all* of myth's functions?

It is perhaps not surprising that, as psychologists, most writers on the topic seem to presume that it is the *psychological function* which is to be addressed by personal myth. A few of the bolder ones incorporate the *metaphysical function* as well, but none go any further. Some nod to the prospect that a new cultural myth is on the horizon, but decline to imagine what it might be or how it might come into being. Even Campbell, content to accept the modern secular world as a kind of "neutral" zone in which individuals work out their myths for themselves, does not venture

---

* Usually dated to the scientific revolution of the 17ᵗʰ century—though, as Campbell observes, "the actual nuclear problem was already present, and recognized by many, at the very peak of that great period of burgeoning French cathedrals (1150–1250)" (*Creative Mythology*, p. 395).

to consider how mythopoesis could re-enchant more than just the personal psyche.

But, what if it can?

Personal myth has the power to transform individual lives, as it did Jung's, by reconnecting them with the mythic forces of meaning, encountered directly. Indeed, in the spiritual desert we inhabit today, this is quickly becoming the *only* authentic, non-regressive path for reclaiming that sense of meaning and coherence which myth once provided. However, just because this kind of myth is *personal*—that is, rooted in our own experience and not within an inherited set of traditions and customs—does not mean that the practice of personal myth needs to be *isolated*, lonely, an entirely subjective affair cut off from community and the rest of the world. Certainly Jung's personal mythmaking had a profound impact on society. What would it look like if personal mythmaking operated *in community*? What if shared and safe spaces existed in which developing your personal myth was cultivated and encouraged? What could *inter*-personal myth look like in such supportive environments? Might they not be the very contexts required for the urgently-needed *new myths* to develop? What if collective, creative mythmaking offered the means, not just to *avoid* our modern spiritual desert, but actually to *replenish* it? What if this task was, collectively, our shared *task of tasks*?

What if re-enchanting the *world* were the great endeavor of our generation? What if transforming God into a new form was the cathedral for our children's?

Here I would like to explore these bold possibilities by traversing the full range of personal myth—to hoist sail and embark out into its still-unnavigated waters: expanding the map of personal mythmaking even *further*, to reveal not just what it is, but—more importantly—what it *could* be. Here I will explore how the meaning from personal mythmaking can extend beyond the individual to create a vast, collective web of inter-personal significance—even to the point of forming a shared, cultural project: the kind of aspirational effort that founds and motivates whole civilizations.

Beginning with more typical personal myth work (focusing first on the *psychological* function, then integrating the *metaphysical* function), we'll see how personal mythmaking can bring a transformative sense of meaning back into modern individual lives. From there, we'll move on, to see how these efforts develop into another level—what I call "creative spirituality"—wherein mythmaking is re-integrated into the communal sphere to address once more our connection to the universe (the *cosmological* function) and to each other (the *sociological* function). Here, a culture of personal mythmaking blends into a new cultural myth—the New Myth some have seen on the horizon, but as yet failed to approach.

A new mythology is waiting to be born, a communal project like never before, in which every individual can take part.

It all begins with us.

DRAFTING

FOUNDATIONS

The quest for myth usually begins after one has experienced a loss of meaning. A state of unquestioned assurance, orientation, and motivation is lost. Only in retrospect can it be seen that you had been living a myth, living *mythologically*—and that this was what had given your life meaning. Without it, you feel unmoored, adrift, without a core and without direction.

Jung spoke of his own crisis of meaning as a period of "inner uncertainty," "disorientation," and the feeling of being "suspended in mid-air"—all commonly-attested sensations. Compare Nietzsche's description of manic disorientation after announcing the death of God:

> Whither are we moving? Away from all suns? Are we not plunging continually? Backward, sideward, forward, in all directions? Is there still any up or down? Are we not straying, as through an infinite nothing? Do we not feel the breath of empty space? Has it not become colder? Is not night continually closing in on us?[1]

Or Tolstoy's description of his crisis:

> I felt that something had broken within me on which my life had always rested, and that I had nothing left to hold on to...[2]

The loss of meaning occasioned by a loss of myth is experienced as a *dissolution of foundations*. A life that was once a coherent whole has been shattered into unrelated fragments without a common reference point. The single, fixed mark according to which everything else was related and assessed has disappeared, and now there is only confusion, radical relativity, and *vertigo*.

Of course, not everyone has this experience. While some undergo the crisis of meaning as a true rupture—a catastrophic break from myth to meaninglessness, with a clear "before" and "after"—for others there is no such fissure. A true grounding in myth was simply *never* a part of their experience to begin with. For a growing number of people, life has always been just a series of fragments, a progression of moments without any real thread connecting them. You did this, then you did that; maybe someday you'll do this other thing; then, you'll die. That's basically what your biography amounts to. It may sound grim, but hey, that's just how it goes. The only unity tying things together is the fact that the same bundle of atoms (i.e., "you") has been experiencing them. Beyond that, there is no cohesion, order, or purpose to it all. For the increasing number of people raised without any myth, the defining experience isn't vertigo, then, but *nausea*; their prophet isn't Nietzsche but Sartre:

> Nothing happens while you live. The scenery changes, people come in and go out, that's all. There are no beginnings. Days are tacked on to days without rhyme or reason, an interminable, monotonous addition.[3]

Either way, vertigo or nausea, a loss of myth or a lifelong deprivation of it, the recognized reality amounts to the same thing: *life is meaningless*. Nothing gives it direction, nothing ties together the disparate strands into some larger design. Everything is fragments without place, pieces without a part to play or a whole to give it all purpose.

How, then, can the fragments become a whole?

This is precisely the first and fundamental task that personal mythmaking addresses. Dan McAdams writes:

> What is a personal myth? First and foremost, it is a special kind of story that each of us naturally constructs to bring together the different parts of ourselves and our lives into a purposeful and convincing whole. ... We attempt, with our story, to make a compelling aesthetic statement. A personal myth is an act of imagination that is a patterned integration of our remembered past, perceived present, and anticipated future.[4]

Here McAdams relates two key features of a personal myth: We might call them the *What* and the *How*.

The **What** is, to reiterate, a special kind of *story*, which brings together the different parts of ourselves and our lives into *a purposeful and convincing whole*: a *patterned integration* of our past, present, and future. That is: an understanding of your life that sees not just a string of episodes, but one unified narrative—a driving purpose behind all of the important events, and not just chance or accident.

The **How** is in the verbs: *construct, attempt, make*—through an *act of imagination*. Note that these are not passive behaviors, but active, intentional, willed. The myth of your life cannot be imparted to you or found out through some kind of analytical or reasoning process. It is not a fact you encounter—it is a story you craft. Understanding and accepting this idea is crucial. It lies at the very heart of the How of personal myth. So let me say a bit more about it.

FINDING THE PLOT: CHOOSING MEANING

A personal myth can only develop after an individual *chooses* to see the events of their life not just as action but as a *plot* that connects those events and renders them meaningful. Without this conscious decision, nothing will happen. Adjusting your orientation to life is the first and most pivotal step in the process. You can't hear the music if you're tuned in to the wrong frequency. What's needed, first and foremost then, is a shift in perspective.

When I was a child I loved to look at books of optical illusions. Sometimes, I'd get stuck on one. I'd stare at it for what seemed like forever, but I still couldn't see anything. Then, all of a sudden, something would *click*. What I'd been seeing as a duck the whole time suddenly became a rabbit! Just like that. Nothing in the image itself had changed—only my perspective on it.

Adopting a meaningful attitude to your life is something like that. Nothing about the facts changes—only one's subjective *relation* to those facts. For example, say you lose your job and are deeply disappointed, then get another job which you like more. Is this how you tell the story? Or do you say that you were *meant* to leave your old job *so that* you could find the new? That you were *supposed to* end up where you did? The facts are the same, only your orientation to them is different. In one telling, the events are simply a disconnected series; in the other, they are *integrated*, one *leading* to the next along a path, with the positive outcome as the *meaning* of it all.

Chances are, you probably know someone who looks at their life like this. Chances are, however, that those people are rather naïve. They assume, without question or doubt, that that's just how the mechanics of the world really work. For them, seeing their lives as leading, by means of some hidden design, from one thing to the next is the consequence of a rather unsophisticated and uncritical worldview. Perhaps they are a fundamentalist whose hidden design is arranged by a personal God. Or they are a New Age guru type whose hidden design is arranged by "the Universe." Such folks are indeed living in a myth, but they have never experienced a loss of it. They do not understand the experience of meaninglessness, either as a product of disillusion or deprivation, vertigo or nausea. For them, meaning is naïve and instinctual. It is something "out there," a force like gravity, that affects the events of their lives.

From the standpoint of true psychological development and personal and spiritual growth, this naiveté is a weakness, not a strength. By remaining ignorant of the condition of meaninglessness, they remain unconscious of the true nature of meaning. Ultimately, naïve meaning is not the same thing as what I aim to describe: meaning as choice, as a *willed decision* to see the events of one's life as purposeful. Such a process does not simply seek to regress back to a state of blissful mythic naiveté, but to move forward, through conscious awareness, towards an even deeper connection with myth and meaning. The crisis of meaning is thus a necessary step on the path toward this fuller integration.

The very fact that you're reading this book suggests you are no stranger to that crisis. As a consequence, you *are* in the position to appreciate the true nature of meaning. Having stepped outside of myth, you have gained the vantage necessary to see it for what it is. Unfortunately, such disillusionment is where too many end their search. The prospect of somehow regaining a sense of mythic meaning *after* critical awareness seems impossible. As you will see, though, this is not only possible, but necessary. It all begins—as so many things do—with that shift in perspective.

For a personal myth to develop, an intention must first be set: you must decide to orient yourself towards meaning, to *choose* meaning. This is the crucial initiatory movement, the *metanoia* (shift in mindset) that sets your consciousness on a new path. From a condition of meaninglessness, one chooses to affirm meaning in their experience—not, however, as something *encountered*, but as something *constructed*.

Adrift in meaninglessness, it is the *will* that breaks the impasse, not the reason.[*] The consequence of this is that meaning, if it is to be found at all, will need to be found *subjectively*, initiated through an act of the will.[†]

COMMITTED VS. CONVINCED

Of course, reflectively *choosing* to see meaning in your life is not the same thing as just immediately seeing it as meaningful. Nor will it feel the same. Simply asserting that your life is a meaningful whole does not suddenly change your perception of it. There is no sudden "aha!" of seeing the duck as a rabbit. In short,

---

[*] It was, after all, the failure of the effort of reason to find meaning objectively "out there" that usually precipitates the state of disillusioned meaninglessness. This is the case collectively (Western disenchantment through secularization), but tends to be the case individually, too (rational reflection leading to doubt and disillusionment).
[†] This was the philosophical insight of the great existentialist thinkers. So, for instance, "truth is subjectivity" for Søren Kierkegaard, who saw in individual choice the crucial movement from despair into the ethical and religious spheres. Perhaps more importantly for us, though, is Nietzsche's articulation of the ideas of "eternal recurrence" and *amor fati* ("love of fate"): the notion that one must affirm one's own life completely, just as it is, embracing necessity as destiny and accident as fortune. Such philosophical principles precisely undergird the orientation one must cultivate in personal mythmaking.

choosing to see your life as meaningful will not immediately mean you find the idea *convincing*.

Etymologically, the meaning of *convincing* is to be "overpowered." One has, as it were, *no option* but to assent to some idea or proposition—you are simply convinced. Try as you might, your mind simply won't allow you to assert that $2 + 2 = 5$. Subjected to the proof, you submit to the force of the argument, and, by compulsion, accept. This is the kind of truth that scientists and many philosophers aim at—logical or axiomatic truth, following clear lines of deductive reasoning that lead, ineluctably and unavoidably, to a single, incontrovertible answer.

But this is not the only kind of truth. There are other realities that require bringing *subjectivity* to bear on determining the truth. Some things require a certain kind of subjective participation to become real. Imagine, for example, that a pair of identical twins has been signed up by their parents to play on a hockey team. One twin loves hockey, but the other hates it. Who will be a better hockey player? Physically speaking, both are equally capable. However, an individual's *passion* for a task will obviously influence their proficiency. Interest, too, is a cause. Here it's the subjective state that proves the determining factor. The psychologist can sometimes answer what the physicist is blind to.

As the pragmatist philosopher William James has noted, our inner orientations and affects do not just respond to truths, but actively shape and condition them. The subjective influences the objective. Take, for example, the question, *Do you like me or not?* "Whether you do or not," says James,

> depends, in countless instances, on whether I meet you half-way, am willing to assume that you must like me, and show you trust and expectation. The previous faith on my part in

your liking's existence is in such cases what makes your liking come. But if I stand aloof, and refuse to budge an inch until I have objective evidence, until you shall have done something apt ... ten to one your liking never comes. ... The desire for a certain kind of truth here brings about that special truth's existence; and so it is in innumerable of other sorts... [Man's] faith acts on the powers above him as a claim, and creates its own verification. ... There are, then, cases where a fact cannot come at all unless a preliminary faith exists in its coming.[5]

So, examining your seemingly incoherent and meaningless life, you choose to assert, "All of this coheres; all of it is meaningful." But you are not convinced. You are, however, *committed*. The experience of meaning, you see, is not in the thing, but in yourself. After a loss of naïve meaning, meaning may not be convincing, but it can be regained as a commitment.

This is true, first, because the proper locus of meaning needs to be grasped: it is an *inner*, psychic condition, not an objective fact. To see it as something objective is to engage in an act of *projection*: the psychological act of assigning an inner state to an outer object.

Projection is a very common psychological process. We do it all the time, and always unconsciously. For example, perhaps you've worked on a home improvement project that isn't going so well. You struggle with your wrench to tighten a bolt that *just won't tighten*. Again and again you try, but completely without success. Finally, face red, sweat beading, you reach a boiling point. Exasperated, you hurl the wrench down on the ground and stomp on it repeatedly, cursing. In reality, of course, this isn't the wrench's fault. But you've projected your inner psychic turmoil outward, onto an object. *My inner frustration* is experienced as

This damn wrench! The two become confused, and, for a moment at least, the wrench is what's bad, not your feelings.

Powerful sentiments very often tend to get caught up in projections. Think, for example, how people relate to a spot where a bad accident occurred. Even if nothing about the place is inherently dangerous, they may pass by it warily, feel "creeped out" by it, or tell people to avoid it. Inner anxieties are thus unwittingly projected outward onto the object, with the object treated as though it were the source and cause of the reaction. Or think about how people relate to their country's flag. Though just a symbol, when "desecrated," it is not uncommon to see people act as though their flag somehow *contains* their country's essence. If sufficiently roused, people can be willing to die for a flag as though it *were* their country—to die for a projection.

The same is true in naïve experiences of meaning. The inner, psychic sense of meaning is projected out of the subject and onto objective reality, as though meaning were something to be found "out there." It's not that I make sense and significance out of what occurs, it's that God/The Universe has arranged things to be significant. It's not that *I feel* a sense of meaning, it's that *life is* meaningful.

After disillusionment, one experiences an understanding that this is not the case, that meaning is *not* so discovered "out there." Such a disillusionment can be occasioned by any number of events, but usually occurs when one attempts to apply objective and rational investigative techniques to their presumed "objects" of meaning. A sense of vocation, one's tenets of faith, the existence of God—such things turn out to be mere phantoms when considered through an objective lens. That is, they are not "out there" to be discovered. That is because they were never objective to begin with, but actually inner, subjective experiences projected out.

Since our horizons have changed so drastically, from those formed by myth to those formed by science, subjective and objective realities have become sharply divided. The objective frame has become the default and dominant frame for modern Western people; subjective realities are, by comparison, considered *less real*, as *merely* subjective. As a result, accepting that meaning is not objective is experienced as akin to saying that meaning is not real.

This is where *choosing* meaning enters in. By requiring the activation of the will—which is to say a conscious focus of the individual's inner psychic energy—the experience of meaning is returned to its properly-recognized domain: the inner, *subjective* domain. The illusion of projection is broken and the source of meaning is correctly identified as coming from "in here," not "out there." The psyche is thus put into a new and more appropriate relationship to the apprehension of meaning. The faulty foundations of meaning built upon projection, which have disintegrated during the meaning crisis, are now rebuilt afresh on firmer ground. The psyche thus finds its ground within itself, not in illusory projections "out there."

Once this is established, the second consequence of this volitional affirmation of meaning begins to take effect: namely, that the experience of meaning is a case where "a fact cannot come at all unless a preliminary faith exists in its coming." If I am dead-set against liking someone, there's no amount of kindness or flattery in the world that they could employ which would change my mind about them. The hypothetical future scenario of us being friends depends entirely upon me first opening myself up to the possibility of my liking them. In a similar way, if I am psychologically committed to the idea that life is meaningless, that everything is just a consequence of chance and necessity, then I have already *chosen* how my existence will be experienced. Indeed, it is very easy to be *convinced* that life is meaningless precisely because the presumption is that meaning is a fact like other facts waiting to be discovered (or not discovered) "out there." When it is inevitably *not* found "out there," my presumptions compel me and I am convinced: life is meaningless.

By asserting meaning through a willful orientation, one can still be *convinced* that life is meaningless even as one becomes *committed* to seeing it as meaningful. In fact, this is the first stage you will need to inhabit after choosing meaning and beginning the task of developing your personal myth. The key here is the effective navigation of a new *attitude* toward meaning and the world, a new orientation to your life.

Because there is an apparent tension between your objective convictions and your subjective commitments, you will need an attitude that can accommodate *both* realities. Such an orientation thus requires holding a "both/and" perspective. Through this perspective, *both* the objective-truth mindset *and* the subjective-truth mindset can coexist. This can be done if you learn to experience things in an "as if" mode. That is, if you can learn to experience them *as if* they were meaningful, *as if* they were connected, etc. While this may sound challenging, even paradoxical, it's actually quite natural.

It's called *play*.

PLAYING TOWARDS MYTH

Both the objective and the subjective mindsets have something crucial to offer us. We need both—the one to keep us from thinking our unconscious projections are "out there," the other to maintain their reality "in here." It is finding a workable relationship between these sometimes-incommensurable frameworks that becomes the challenge. As Jung experienced when he allowed powerful psychic material to well up from within, madness is never far from mythic meaning. As he observed, "the fund of unconscious images which fatally confuse the mental patient" is also "the matrix of a mythopoeic imagination which had vanished from our rational age." How do we break the dam of that mythopoeic imagination without losing ourselves in our own fantasy worlds? As D. Stephenson Bond reflects in his book *Living Myth: Personal Meaning as a Way of Life*:

> Objective consciousness has freed us from the tyranny of projection. Will it also forever imprison the imagination? That is the modern dilemma. With too little objective consciousness, we live in the tyranny of the unconscious—the loss of soul that makes us crazy. We are lost in a complete identification with the object. Yet with too much objective consciousness, we live the tyranny of objectivity—the loss of soul that makes us neurotic, for the loss of imagination is also the loss of soul. When you can't feel the tug in your psyche toward a [magic] stone, something essential is lost: a connection, a sense of meaning, an imaginative spark. The touch of myth.[6]

How, then, are we to regain the touch of myth without losing touch with objective reality? As McAdams suggested, the best way to engage this mindset is through an "act of imagination." That is, we must learn, as Jung did on the beach, *to play*.

Play activates the infinite possibilities of the imagination within a set frame. It carves out of objective consciousness a demarcated zone, a special space or field for fantasy. When someone playing says that they're Superman, we don't worry that they've slipped out of reality into a psychotic state or lost all sense of reality. We know, and they know, that this playful attitude is operating with half an eye open to objective reality. They *are* Superman—but only within the field of play carved out of an objective reality that continues to exist in the background, and to which they can return as necessary. When applied to our lives, Bond calls this kind of playful mindset "symbolic consciousness":

> Symbolic consciousness... participates in the subjective process of fantasy while at the same time maintaining awareness of the process as an objective, autonomous factor. In other words, it lives in a myth while knowing it as a myth; it experiences the fantasy process neither as "reality" nor "illusion," but rather as *meaning*. ... The trick of symbolic consciousness is in allowing yourself to maintain the distance—I am aware that I'm pretending, gaming, imagining—while at the same time preserving participation.[7]

Symbolic consciousness is unlike the fundamentalist's and guru's naïve engagements with mythic thinking mentioned earlier; but it is also unlike the critical, objective mindset that causes such naiveté to collapse into meaninglessness. The reason? Symbolic consciousness is *volitional*—one *chooses* to engage in it and is thus aware of the framework. By contrast, naiveté isn't chosen; meaning is simply accepted as a given (i.e., one believes the projection). Critical objectivity is also not chosen; one is *convinced* by its evidence and arguments—even, perhaps, while kicking and screaming—to abandon mythic thinking (i.e., one recognizes the projection as such and rejects it as illusory). Symbolic consciousness, however, *chooses* to engage in mythic thinking, but in a knowing state of play. One acts *as if* it were true. Bond writes:

> As in a ball game, "I" have to assent and participate if this imaginative game is to develop. I have to "allow" my ego to play, assent to the fantasy that forms, and play as if the game were real—as if three strikes really means I'm out, and an imaginary line really means fair and foul. ... You have to allow yourself to "get into" the game as if it is important. Then you enter symbolic consciousness. If you let go, you enjoy the game.[8]

Critical awareness thus remains—it simply does not run the show. Recall Jung's critical self-awareness as, reconnecting with his inner child, he played with stones. *"Now, really, what are you about?"* it demanded. *"You are building a small town, and doing it as if it were a rite!"* It's easy to imagine him giving up right then and there, heading home embarrassed with himself and never mentioning the episode again. Instead, Jung heard this reflective critique from himself—but continued developing his myth anyway.

In playing towards myth, one must choose to believe in the face of disbelief. You choose to believe. While that might sound like a paradox, it really isn't as hard as it seems. We do it every time we watch a movie or, well, a *play*! For an audience, the so-called "suspension of disbelief" is crucial for the drama's magic to work. No one needs to be told how to do this; it just comes naturally to us.

Such an attitude, then, is not just some tortured mechanism for disenchanted moderns to find their way back to myth. Rather, according to Joseph Campbell, something like this mindset lies at the very core of mythic engagement. For example, in many traditional or tribal cultures, special festivals are held, during which masked dancers celebrate mythic rites. It is understood that, during these dances, the participants do not just *act like* the gods and goddesses, but actually *become* them in some meaningful way. Campbell says of their serious play:

> there has been a shift of view from the logic of the normal secular sphere, where things are understood to be distinct from one another, to a theatrical or play sphere, where they are accepted for what they are *experienced* as being and the logic is that of "make believe"—"as if." ...Such a highly played game of "as if" frees our mind and spirit...from the bondage of reason... [A] principle of release operates throughout the series by way of the alchemy of an "as if"; and that, through this, the impact of so-called "reality" upon the psyche is transubstantiated. The play state and the rapturous seizures sometimes deriving from it represent, therefore, a step rather *toward* than away from the ineluctable truth; and belief—acquiescence in a belief that is not quite belief—is the first step toward the deepened participation... [9]

Campbell refers to this as a process of "self-induced belief," and it remains the way back to living water in our spiritual desert. Through play, one can discover a "second naivete," in which the power of myth can again be allowed to work without a loss of conscious awareness about objective reality. Moreover, such play states can actually move us *closer* to reality, properly understood—a comprehensive reality beyond just lop-sided objectivity. Play opens us to bigger truths.

It is within such an imaginative and creative state that one must cast their gaze on the raw material of their experience and seek the myth in it. Like a kid gazing up at the clouds and seeing pictures, look back at who you've been and what you've done and seek the bigger picture. Let it take shape...

What is the *story* of your life? What are its decisive moments? Who are its main characters? What are its themes, its motifs, its potent symbols? So gazing, all that you are now comes into play. Your life is your canvas. And even failures, losses, and disasters have their significance. To become who you are, nothing was for naught. Even the worst betrayals and wounds—suffered, or inflicted—everything, through story, is redeemed, insofar as it communicates who you've become and marks the stages on your way. You stand today on a path you have been walking your whole life, much of it unwittingly. You were destined to be here, and it is now clear that your experience conspired to put you exactly where you are—*in order to get you where you're going.*

So where is that? Your story has a destination it's been driving at—which means you have a goal, an aim, a purpose. What is it? When you hit upon an answer to this question—one you like, one that works for you, that speaks to the warp and weft of your experience and directs it toward some goal—you'll have put your finger on *your personal myth.*

Seen in this light, in the light of mythic meaning, nothing is wasted, nothing unnecessary. Everything *matters.* In this way, one can feel what Nietzsche meant when he wrote:

> Throw off your discontent about your nature. Forgive yourself your own self. You have it in your power to merge everything you have lived through—false starts, errors, delusions,

passions, your loves and your hopes—into your goal, with nothing left over.[10]

Try it.

Imagine purpose in your life. Pretend, if only for a moment, that things don't "just happen," but happen "for a reason." That reason is *you*—who you are and where you're headed. Make believe that, like a novel or a movie, there's a plot you're playing out—a running thread that strings together the many varied beads of your experience into a work of art, a "compelling aesthetic statement." You didn't know it then, but the events that set you on your course were laden with significance. As in a novel, there's symbolism and foreshadowing—once you know what to look for. As in a great story, there's a design—once you've gained the proper perspective on it ("only afterward did I see how all the parts fitted together").

Most books on personal myth include exercises to help you do just this, since the process can take time and require some guidance. For this, different writers employ different methods. These include writing prompts (Keen and Valley-Fox; Feinstein and Krippner; Slattery), biographical interviews (McAdams), guided meditations (Feinstein and Krippner), mask-making (Larsen), studying/meditating on traditional myths (Campbell, Chalquist), dream incubation/analysis (Feinstein and Krippner), and others. Such methods are diverse, but all alike in requiring that you activate your imagination through a playful state. Ultimately, though, while such books and exercises may guide you, no one can tell you what your personal myth is. Only *you* can do that.

LIVING MYTH

Once you've drafted your personal myth—fleshed out its narrative arc, hit upon its themes and motifs, envisioned a direction or goal to which it aims—there remains a final step. You must *live it*. Or, better put, you must *live into it*. Meaning is an orientation, a temperament, a proclivity, not just some creed or fact you passively accept. It is a way of life. Living your myth thus requires continual participation, always choosing the significant interpretation, always acting "as if" your myth is true. It means directing your behavior and activities in service of the end to which you've chosen to believe your life aims.

Like all activities regularly tended to, such things do not stay challenging for long. In time, if diligently performed, these choices will become habit—habit, as the saying goes, becomes character, and character becomes destiny. That is, from your commitment, a *new sense of conviction* can develop. Will and experience so fuse and inform one another, that myth and reality, the subjective and objective, harmonize. The dichotomy is synthesized, and only wholeness remains.

It is to this reclaimed sense of wholeness and meaning that personal myth leads. In the end, if you are able to shift your perspective and choose meaning, construct a story that integrates the different parts of your life into a purposeful and convincing whole through a play-like act of imagination, and live into that story as if it were indeed true, you will have succeeded in recentering yourself in myth.

Specifically, personal myth at this level succeeds in fulfilling myth's **psychological function**, one of the four functions of myth mentioned above. Campbell writes that the goal of the psychological function is "the centering and unfolding of the individual in integrity,"[11] carrying them through the stages of their life development in such a way as "to harmonize and deepen the psyche."[12] Or, as summarized earlier: *to center the individual, carry them through the stages of development, and harmonize them with their world.*

A working personal myth does this by rebuilding the foundations of a purposeful life and providing a sense of meaning and direction to one's development. Such a life is no longer at odds with existence (i.e., either in vertigo or nausea), but acceptingly embraces the world as the stage for unfolding meaning. The troubled psyche—adrift, anxious, unmotivated— here finds relief. A new center is established, providing orientation and a basis of value. So all the increasingly pervasive symptoms of modern alienation—depression, anxiety, uncertainty, a sense of worthlessness, etc.—find a pathway to healing.

As I've said, most of the books written on personal myth since Jung focus on this sort of foundational work. And that makes sense. Modern people have been growing ever more estranged from myth as time goes by. With so much disillusionment, and so few compelling solutions, it is no easy task to reconnect with living myth and meaning in today's world. Initiation is required—in a time of fewer and fewer genuine initiators.

But, once you've found your footing, so to speak, and are no longer so "suspended in mid-air," you can begin to explore the landscape of myth a bit more and go still deeper. Having made a purposeful whole of your life, you will have developed a taste for myth—but there is more, *much* more, for those willing to keep up their serious play.

THE BLUEPRINT

FINDING THE ALTAR

Now really, what are you about? You've constructed a whole story out of your life as though it were a myth!

Yes, you say, that is exactly what you've done. But perhaps you've actually done more than that. Perhaps that's just the beginning. For, if you really think about it, is your meaningful story now your myth or is myth now your meaningful story? Some further looking inward will get at what I mean by this.

In his writing about personal myth, Joseph Campbell came up with a very helpful and revealing "test" for helping people uncover what their own driving myth may be. He writes:

> You might ask yourself this question: if I were confronted with a situation of total disaster, if everything I loved and thought I lived for were devastated, what would I live for? If I were to come home, find my family murdered, my house burned up, or all my career wiped out by some disaster or another, what would sustain me? ...What would lead me to know that I could go on living and not just crack up and quit? I've known religious people who have had such experiences. They would say, "It's God's will." For them, faith would work. Now, what do you have in your life that would play this role for you?[1]

How you answer this question, Campbell says, "That is the test of the myth, the building myth, of your life."[2]

Campbell's test is insightful at all stages of developing a personal myth. If you're having trouble identifying what your driving story really is, it's worth asking this question and seeing what arises inside you.

But the implications of Campbell's question go deeper than that. Let's say you've already experienced such a crisis—and even found, on the other side, a new meaning to bring the pieces back together. Your faith collapsed—but you found a new myth. Your meaning disappeared, but you forged anew. Good for you. But... what if *that* falls apart? What happens when, using the methods discussed above, you've constructed a new story and then *that* gets torn to pieces? You'd thought you'd gotten things all sorted out once you chose to see that divorce as meaningful: it all led to your *new* relationship, after all. Well, what do you do when your *second* husband leaves, or unexpectedly passes away? What do you do when the cancer comes back? When your addict partner relapses? When redemption stalls?

What do you do *when your personal myth fails?*

Some people are unlucky enough to have their world crumble only once. However, if you've truly learned the art of mythmaking, of transforming accident into design, you will know what meaning's really made of; you will be *immune* to despair. Why?

*"The readiness is all."**

Meaning isn't in the events, but in your *relationship* to them. It's in the orientation you choose, the perspective you take. It's in the *will*, and nothing external can take that from you. If your world is rocked, if your story falls apart, you are not adrift; you have the power to enchant tragedy, no matter what. Your story is not your myth: *myth is your story.*

"God's will." *Amor fati.*† Destiny. These are mythic attitudes that allow you to *accept what is*; to *affirm* your life, *as it is,*

---

* *Hamlet*, Act 5, Scene 2.
† "The love of fate."

whatever happens; to say *Yes* to being you, *Yes* to your biography, whatever it may bring. To make of accident (or anything) a basis for your mission. Life it is—*your* life, and, as such, it *shall* be meaningful.

Well, as it happens, *you're* the only one in the position to make that proclamation. No one else determines it. It's up to you to gild disaster with significance, and raise from worthless happenstance to Calling what befalls you on the world's wide heath.

If you can do this—if you can wrench out of catastrophe the unexpected acorn of your myth and make a myth out of catastrophe—then myth has served you in the deepest way of all. It has shot through everything, *everything*, with a shiver of transcendence. Meaning is in the making. God is in the overcoming—not in the myth you overcame.

Such ability to mythologize moves you beyond just the storytelling of a cohesive life, and thus beyond the "psychological" sphere alone. Far more than that, this is an engagement with living myth that performs the first and foremost function of mythology—the **metaphysical function**: the great Yes to the Greatest Question.

Campbell writes:

The first function [of myth] is awakening in the individual a sense of awe and mystery and gratitude for the ultimate mystery of being. In the old traditions – the very old ones – the accent was on *saying yea to the world as it is*. That's not easy...[3]

This means saying Yes, even to the devastated life; Yes, to total disaster. Yes, to all of it, just as it is.

Campbell refers to this ability to say "yes" to life as a "reconciliation" of the self and reality. Thus, elsewhere he calls the metaphysical function of myth the power "to reconcile consciousness with existence,"[4] or that it deals with "the problem of reconciling consciousness to the preconditions of its own experience, which is to say to life."[5] Ultimately, it is this capacity to become reconciled to existence *as it is* that allows you to transform your life—from vertigo or nausea into meaning and myth.

The world is what it is, and, like God at creation, you look at it and declare "it is good!" For to affirm the world is to affirm your life, and vice versa. To be able to look on all the seeming chaos and confusion, the wild and profound forces propelling everything on, the overwhelming immensity of what you find yourself now pitted against, now crushed beneath, now riding upon in grandeur—to look at this great, incomprehensible enormity of what is in true acceptance, *that* is the unshakable Ground from which all meaning springs. To find this stance is to find the Archimedean point outside all fear and resentment, tireless longing and simmering disappointment. It is the Yes that makes your life, *all* life, mythical—shot through with the glory of God, incontrovertible. Campbell writes:

> And this yea itself is the released energy that bears us beyond loathing and desire, breaks the barriers of rational judgment and unites us with our own deep ground: the "secret cause."[6]

Such a recognition shifts the fundamental orientation of personal myth. It is no longer your own creative ability to imagine your disparate experiences as a cohesive whole that renders them meaningful. This imaginative effort has expanded—into an

38

appreciation of *the universe itself* as such a whole, one into which your own life fits and has its part and place. To affirm your life as destiny is to affirm *all* happening as destiny, to affirm *all* the workings of existence as some great Story—even if one too far beyond one's own small reckoning to comprehend.

And yet, though incomprehensible, it is also a "compelling aesthetic statement," the *ultimate* work of art, in fact, which strikes your heart and compels your wonder—so much so, that even though you cannot tell the plot, your wonder by itself is enough for it to earn your affirmation and deserve your Yes.

"Only a few days before his death," recounts the great Jungian analyst and writer Edward Edinger in his book *Ego and Archetype*, Carl Jung

> was asked by an interviewer about his notion of God. He replied in these words: "To this day God is the name by which I designate all things which cross my willful path violently and recklessly, all things which upset my subjective views, plans and intentions and change the course of my life for better or worse." The view Jung is here expressing is essentially a primitive view, albeit a conscious and sophisticated one. Jung is calling "God" what most people call chance or accident. He experiences apparently arbitrary happenings as meaningful rather than meaningless. ...For the Self-connected man...chance does not exist.[7]

Personal myth at this level thus operates in a way that fulfills not only the psychological function of myth (*to center the individual, carry them through the stages of development, and harmonize them with their world*) but also the *metaphysical function: to awaken in the individual a sense of awe and gratitude for the Ultimate Mystery, reconciling them to reality as it is.*

Look how far play can take you! From saying Yes to the story of our lives to saying Yes to the Story of existence. From finding a ground within to a Ground beyond ourselves and in all things. In this way, what Campbell says about the high art of tragedy applies also to the art of personal mythmaking (indeed, perhaps they are essentially the same). After considering this Yes-saying stance, he writes:

> Thus a breakthrough is accomplished from biography to metaphysics, the backdrop of time dissolves and the prospect opens of an occult power shaping our lives that is at once of the universe and of each of us, a *mysterium tremendum et fascinans*, which is finally that everlasting fire which is exploding in the galaxies, blazing in the sun, reflected in the moon, and coursing as the ache of desire through our veins.[8]

What is this *"mysterium tremendum et fascinans"* Campbell refers to when talking about the metaphysical function of myth? The term comes from the great German scholar of religion Rudolf Otto, specifically his work *The Idea of the Holy*. The book is about the so-called *"numinous* experience"—that distinct feeling, typical of religious experiences, when a person feels connected with the true ground of all things, the ultimate mystery at the core of reality, which is both terrible/tremendous and fascinating (*tremendum et fascinans*). Such a feeling, Otto writes,

> may at times come sweeping like a gentle tide, pervading the mind with a tranquil mood of deepest worship. It may pass over into a more set and lasting attitude of the soul,

continuing, as it were, thrillingly vibrant and resonant, until at last it dies away and the soul resumes its "profane," non-religious mood of everyday experience. It may burst in sudden eruption up from the depths of the soul with spasms and convulsions, or lead to the strangest excitements, to intoxicated frenzy, to transport, and to ecstasy. ...It may become the hushed, trembling, and speechless humility of the creature in the presence of—whom or what? In the presence of that which is a *mystery* inexpressible and above all creatures.[9]

Such feelings characterize the encounter with the *mysterium tremendum et fascinans*—the sense of the Ultimate. In the final analysis, life is affirmed because of its connection to this Ultimate Reality, before which we stand in wonder and awe and gratitude. In the ultimate analysis, to affirm your life is to affirm this Ultimate Reality, which is the great Mystery. It is to *this* that your self stands in relation; it is within this that you live your life. It is therefore this glorious Mystery which *sanctifies* your life, which compels your affirmation at a non-rational level. Indeed—even to *identify* with that Mystery, to personalize it. You yourself are also an expression of that same Mystery. As Campbell was always fond of saying, quoting the Hindu mystics: "*Thou art that.*" So the first function of myth is for a man to stand before the awe-full Mystery of life—"not to be afraid of it, but to recognize it is his own mystery dimension as well."[10]

And so your mythmaking has progressed to this—from an infusion of your own existence with meaning, to a recognition of that same meaning in all of existence, in all that exists: from *personal* myth, you might say, to personal *myth*.

The big, cultural myths once served to communicate this "numinous" aspect of existence to individuals. This was, in fact, the very essence of religion and religious practice. It is what the given tradition's mythic symbols achieved. Christ on the cross, Buddha under the Bo Tree, Krishna in Arjuna's chariot. All triggered a response to the numinous, to the holy. As living myths, they worked to put people in touch with the *mysterium tremendum* by activating certain psychic states.

With the decline of traditional religions though, this, too, is now left to the individual, to discover the link and articulate it in personally meaningful terms—that is, as personal myth. So Bond writes:

> When the cultural expression of the relationship to psyche itself is no longer sustaining the myth-creating process must unfold along the lines of an individual relationship to the impersonal psyche. A new expression of the functional relationship is required; a religious expression in the individual that emerges from careful and scrupulous observation of the *numinosum* in his or her own life—an individual religious practice.[11]

In this way, the task of personal mythmaking deepens, moving beyond expressing one's experience *as* myth to expressing one's experience *of* myth—from building a meaningful whole out of your life to articulating your life in relation to the meaningful Whole. Put differently, personal myth at this level will entail your own personal articulation of the holy, the numinous, the *mysterium tremendum*. So it is that personal myth leads naturally to the development of a *personal spirituality*—indeed, to something like a *personal religion*.

MATERIALS

THE HUMBLE HOLY

But...the *holy*? Where does one even begin? As before, the answers must come, ultimately, from yourself, your own experience. Sam Keen, a popularizer of the concept of personal myth in the late 20th century and someone who worked with Joseph Campbell on the topic, expressed this idea succinctly. "If I am to discover the holy," he wrote,

> it must be in *my* biography and not in the history of Israel. If there is a principle which gives unity and meaning to history it must be something I touch, feel, and experience. Our starting point must be radical. ... *Is there anything on the native ground of my own experience—my biography, my history—which testifies to the reality of the holy?*[1]

Finding the holy or sacred in your life doesn't necessarily mean you have to have some transcendent mystical experience or daily communion with spirits. Start small. Remember: our disenchanted modern world has become so alienated from any sense of the numinous that it can feel like working an atrophied muscle. All that you've done so far to develop your mythopoeic imagination, though, has put you on your way. Through cultivating a "symbolic consciousness" and learning to keep the objective and the imaginative worlds in proper conversation, you are now much better tuned to, in the words of the poet A. R. Ammons, "consider the radiance" of the world as it is.

In *A Religion of One's Own: A Guide to Creating a Personal Spirituality in a Secular World*, Thomas Moore proposes some modest ideas for fostering your own personally-attuned sense of the sacred. "In developing a religion of one's own," he writes,

> it's important to cultivate an eye for the numinous, a sacred light within things or an aura around them, the feeling that there is more to the world than what meets the eye. You don't have to be naïve or literal about this; it's simply a capacity in human beings to catch a glimpse of the infinite in the finite world, or deep vitality and meaning in what would otherwise be hollow and only material.[2]

You've already practiced this sort of sensibility in relation to your biographical history. It is the imaginative art of seeing more than accident in what occurs, something more *intentional, significant,* a *deeper purpose.* As with your biography, this does not mean becoming "naïve" about objective reality. Nor does it entail white-washing away the hardship and apparent negativity of life. Rather, it means decidedly embracing existence, including the darkness, as meaning-full—part-and-parcel of the same great power unfolding in all that is. When you consider the radiance of the whole of existence with such a pair of eyes, writes Ammons,

> then
> the heart moves roomier, the man stands and looks about, the
>
> leaf does not increase itself above the grass, and the dark
> work of the deepest cells is of a tune with May bushes
> and fear lit by the breadth of such calmly turns to praise.*

A personal articulation of this power—this *mysterium* at the heart of being, which has held your greatest, most sublime moments and also, as Ammons says, floods the bones of birds,

---

* From "The City Limits."

looks into the guiltiest swervings of the heart, and illuminates the bodies of the flies that feast on shit and carrion—such an articulation must eventually become the task of personal mythmaking.

For many, this radiance shines through in those great transitional moments: births and deaths, each one bounded by the transcendent. Or perhaps other pivotal events have been similar: the day you met or married your partner, had some transformative spiritual insight, acquired a life-changing injury, or found some meaningful forgiveness or redemption. Otherwise, less profound but still significant events can shine with the numinous: synchronicities, welcome breakthroughs, or an unexpected and seemingly impossible serenity amidst a tumultuous time.

SALVAGE AND RECLAIM

According to Jung and Campbell, an intuitive sense of the numinous is instinctual in every human being. All it needs is the proper stimulus to become activated. Certain settings and images work in just this way to evoke the sense of the numinous—we only need to open ourselves to them. Jung famously called these psychological instincts the *archetypes of the unconscious*—essentially, patterned responses lying latent within us, which are triggered by engagement with associated forms. Such was the function that mythological symbols and rituals served in the past. And, though no longer operative as part of a comprehensive tradition, they can still function to varying degrees today, and thereby serve as guides. The development of a *personal* sense of the sacred and numinous does not mean that such traditional mythic forms are irrelevant, that they should play no part or that tradition should be ignored or rejected. Rather, we must learn to use what we have as best we can.

As T. S. Eliot wrote in the early 20th century, we live in a waste land littered by "a heap of broken images." It has become virtually impossible now to inhabit a comprehensive mythic cosmos as humans once did. What we can do, however, is look through the heap of images history has left us in an attempt to *build anew*. While these mythologies no longer function as complete and effective mythic systems, their images and symbols can still speak to us as helpful *aids*: breadcrumbs, you might say, to a working personal expression of the divine. Engaging with them can still stir the archetypal patterns lying latent within, and help awaken your dormant sense of the numinous.

Imagine entering the ruins of a temple from a long-lost civilization. You walk around the courtyard of tumbled pillars covered in ivy. In the bas reliefs carved there, you can make out scenes of gods and goddesses. You don't know their names or their stories, the full dynamics of their sacred epic, but you feel stirred, somehow, nonetheless. You walk up the stairs and enter a small enclosure. Somehow, you know, this was the inner sanctum, the holy of holies. You feel a shudder, a significance, a solemnity, though you don't know why or what of. On the ground lie a broken chalice and some strange figurines. You pick them up and hold them in your hand. You can never know how these were once used, what ritual they spoke to, how they integrated all the pieces of a robust cultural myth into a powerful Story, but you find them infinitely compelling nonetheless. Clearly, the artisan who worked them succeeded in capturing something powerful. The myth is gone, but the symbols still speak, if only faintly, yet still movingly.

Historically, it has been the case that new temples were built on the sites of the old. New gods, even whole new religions may come through—but the sacred site remains. Such things are still powerful, even when the specific Story behind them has been stripped away. The place is rededicated; a pagan temple becomes a church becomes a mosque. But something is preserved—the inherent numinous character. Symbols are reinterpreted, if only so their evocative nature can continue to work in a new context.

So is it for us today. The Old Myths are dimming, their Stories no longer working to cohere a livable mythic narrative we can inhabit. But their many pieces persist—vestiges of numinous encounters, relics of engagements with the unconscious.

As Campbell sees it, a sensitive engagement with such materials is the *best* method one can use to discover and develop your own personal myth. He writes:

> The way to find your own myth is to determine those traditional symbols that speak to you and use them, you might say, as bases for meditation. Let them work on you. …Let them play on the imagination, activating it. By bringing your own imagination into play in relation to these symbols, you will be experiencing…the symbols' power to open a path to the heart of mysteries.[3]

What mythic symbols speak to you? Perhaps it's the mandala. The Earth Goddess. The rustic Pan. The dying-and-rising god. The nine orders of the angelic hierarchy. The paradisal garden. The dragon-slayer. The Great Mother. The divine man. *Whatever* draws you, meditate on such images. Allow your mind to play with them. Imagine new configurations and associations. Let the divine players dance…

Of course, traditional religions are more than just systems of mythic symbols. They contain a plethora of materials, such as ethical teachings, life wisdom, mental and bodily practices, distinct artforms, and communal rituals. All of these can be the source of inspiration and an evocation of the numinous sensibility in you. Moore reflects:

> When you decide to create your own religion, you will want to study the traditions of the formal religions with a fervor you've never known before. You'll discover how valuable they are and how much beauty and wisdom lie in their art and texts and stories and rituals and holy images. You'll want to learn from Buddhist sutras and the Gospel teachings and the Sufi poets and the sayings of Lao Tzu and Chuang Tzu. You will be amazed at the beautiful precision of the Kabbalah and the acute spiritual sensitivity of the Qur'ān—all because you know what it's like to search for spiritual insight and express your spiritual feelings.[4]

For most people who live their lives within a particular religious tradition—Christianity, Buddhism, Islam, etc.—there is no choice here. They must accept what their tradition has given them—and reject other traditions. The canon is set, the dogma is handed down. One can either take it or leave it.

Crucially, this is *not* the case for someone developing a *personal* mythology. Unlike those who practice within such traditional religions, you are not *bound* to any one of them or even any element therein. You are free to play the curator—to listen to your heart and see what genuinely speaks to it. From *this* you craft your vision. Take what works; leave what doesn't. "It makes a big difference," writes Moore,

> whether you feel free to borrow this wisdom or feel you have to buy into it. … Don't take the traditions as they're offered. Struggle with them, work hard at extracting only what is valuable in them, and be ready to discard the dross.[5]

Perhaps a moral saying in one of the Gospels strikes a chord: "Judge not, lest ye be judged." This moves you, resonates as profound and speaks to a truth at your core. Take it into your myth. Conversely, "whoever marries a divorced woman commits adultery" lands with a thud. Leave it. Your heart will tell you the path to take toward the sacred. Conscience, not dogmatic orthodoxy, is your criterion; beauty, not canonical status, is your guide. Campbell writes:

> an intelligent "making use" not of one mythology only but of all the dead and set-fast symbologies of the past, will enable the individual to anticipate and activate in himself the centers of his own creative imagination, out of which his own myth and life-building "Yes because" may then unfold. But in the end, as in the case of Parzival, the guide within will be his own noble heart alone, and the guide without, the image of beauty, the radiance of divinity, that awakes in his heart *amor*: the deepest, inmost seed of his nature, consubstantial with the process of the All... [6]

Let the calling of your subjective imagination lead you. At the same time, don't let it entirely dictate the show either. Listen also to objective insight as well. Unlike mythologies of the past, yours is being made wittingly, in the full sun of conscious awareness. This, too, can be a tool. Follow your heart, but accept input from your mind as well—as all good play allows. Note that an archetypal symbol might resonate with you, but also weigh critically the implications of following it. Not all archetypes, when activated, trigger a divine calm or compassion, a healthy Yes or a sacred ecstasy. And while it is important not to shun the darkness, it is also not ideal to "give the devil a foothold." As Jung noted in *The Archetypes of the Collective Unconscious*, powerful and destructive ideologies such as Nazism, too, activated deep archetypal forces. A psychology plagued by pathological shame might resonate powerfully with the "Fall of Man" trope; a narcissist, perhaps, with Promethean hubris. So be careful. *Probate spiritus* ("test the spirits"), as Jung was fond of quoting. Developing personal myth requires the application of conscious decision-making as well as the tug of fantasy.

Daniele Bolelli is a writer whose works include a cheeky but often earnest and insightful book called *Create Your Own Religion*. In describing the process of doing just that, Bolelli writes:

> We can observe the historical consequences of certain beliefs, and decide which ones have had more desirable effects on our lives. … In creating our own religions, we should carefully separate those ideas that have contributed to the amount of violence, conflict, and suffering in the world from those that have helped alleviate or diminish those things.[7]

This seems like sound advice, and a natural consequence of conscious mythmaking. Indeed, we find ourselves at a unique stage in human history, when the development of myth has entered a phase wherein the worst elements of the human psyche need no longer find unquestioning acceptance simply because of the authority of tradition. Put rather simplistically, traditional myth had offered meaning, but at the often-destructive expense of critical awareness; modern rationalism has offered the critical awareness to avoid such destructive behavior, but often at the expense of meaning. Conscious mythmaking takes the best of both, with the potential to offer both meaning and a constructive orientation to life.

OLD WINE SKINS

Working with mythic symbols can be a good way to connect the conscious and unconscious worlds and open your imagination for numinous experience. In this way, symbols act as mediators between you and the *numinosum*. They are a bridge, a conduit, a translation between it and you. However, there are also categories of experience where the connection is more *immediate* and *direct*. Bond calls such high-intensity ruptures "core experiences," and these can become the grain of sand around which the pearl of your personal myth grows. It can be very helpful to have the traditional symbols to look to after such experiences. Often, they can play the mediators in the other direction—not in translating the numinous to you through culture, but in translating the numinous *back* to the culture through you.

Say one has an ineffable numinous experience. The usual way such an experience gets communicated, if it does at all, is by translating it into the given religious or mythic language of one's culture. This is a big part of the reason why Christians who have visionary experiences express those visions as being of Christ; Buddhists, of Buddha, etc. The culture provides the framework and the symbols by means of which numinous experiences can be meaningfully integrated into the world.

However, much is always lost in translation. A given language imposes its own limits, and sometimes the cultural framework available is not really adequate to the task of communicating a personal core experience. For instance, Bond relates the story of a woman whose core experience involved a profound early-morning encounter with crows, for whom she felt compelled to dance, and by whom she was then led to a mighty oak tree. The experience was personal and profound—but attempting to integrate its religious quality into her life and culture poses a challenge. Was this a "Christian" experience? A "Native" one? What happens if no preexisting label properly applies? What if there is simply no way to "convert" the experience into pre-given forms? "The claim of the crows on this woman," writes Bond,

> has the beginnings of a personal religion. To make a statement, even to herself, about what happened to her, she has to put it in a framework. She needs the frame that tells her how to relate to this experience, that is to say she needs a religious myth to guide her in the relationship to her living psyche. Dancing for the crows was a religious experience, a numinous experience. It forms a core experience. … She may attempt to put it in a cultural religious frame. This woman, for instance, may embrace Native American mythology rather than having to labor over a personal myth. Often nowadays people turn to religious forms and practices outside of their own culture. We do not know if such a "conversion" will be adequate to the claim. The difficulty with conversion has to do with the restless urge of psyche to know itself ever more fully. Where the potential of the individual relationship to psyche exceeds the potential of the culture—any culture, ancient or living—the ground is set for the individuation process to unfold.[8]

In short, our core experiences of the numinous may not "fit" with any given symbol or system. To attempt to force them to does violence to the very thing that makes it what it is, what makes it special. In this way, cultural myths and religions often act as a Procrustean Bed for our own numinous experiences. It is new wine in old wine skins; trying to mix them causes both to be ruined.

In such instances, rather than force the fit, we should learn instead to speak *our own novel mythic language.* To do so, we will need to move beyond tradition, having by now hopefully integrated the insights of its rich treasuries of myths and symbols into our imagination for inspiration. Now, we will need to do something even more challenging than building anew out of the old. Now, we will need to *create mythic imagery.* Larsen writes:

> It is an open question... whether the true meaning of personal mythology is simply to discover that we are repeating a traditional mythic pattern or, as Yeats suggested, that we are in touch with a still-alive "supernatural," which requires us to create new mythologies with the very stuff of our lives. If we are searching for patterns, we must rely on our reading of myths. If we must create new myths to live by, however, knowing traditional myths may be helpful but not enough. What new thing may be required of us is as yet unknown; but we may find that the answer lies only in the living.[9]

Here the road diverges somewhat. The aim to "create new myths to live by"—what Joseph Campbell called "creative mythology"—is not for everyone, but rather is to be pursued by "an adequate individual, loyal to his own experience of value."[10] Instead of mining the past for materials, these mythmakers must forge entirely new bricks out of their own imaginations, intuitions, and experiences if they are to build their cathedral. In so doing, they may just offer something for *all* of us.

CONSTRUCTION

BREAKING GROUND

Ultimately, a creative mythology built from personal mythmaking is both an engagement with universal archetypes as well as a highly unique and idiosyncratic vision of a particular mind. Like a fingerprint, they are common to all humans, but no one is the same. Speaking to this distinctive aspect, Campbell compares creative myths to portraits of their mythmaker, revealing their personal essence, rooted in their own time and place of the world *as it is*. "A great portrait," he says in *Creative Mythology*,

> is a revelation, through the "empirical," of the "intelligible" character of a being whose ground is beyond our comprehension. The work is an icon, so to say, of a spirituality true to this earth and to its life, where it is in the creatures of this world that the Delectable Mountains of our Pilgrim's Progress are discovered, and where the radiance of the City of God is recognized as Man.[1]

In personal myth, the universal and particular collide. According to thinkers like Jung and Campbell, what links them is the *unconscious*, which is both personal and transpersonal, individual and collective. As such, creative myths are able to evoke the universal numinous by means of entirely novel and unique symbols.

Our psyches are teeming with such inchoate images. Abiding just below the surface of consciousness are a whole host of psychic figures and personas: parts of your own personality, it turns out, just waiting to be engaged. A bit deeper and one encounters the great inherited archetypes, which need only the right symbolic representation to become activated in conscious awareness. It is the task of the creative imagination to do just this.

Initiating contact with such bedrock forces can be done in various ways. Dreams, active imagination, fantasy thinking, meditative trances, psychedelics/entheogens, mystical rapture, out-of-body experiences and the like can all produce profound and often transformative spiritual experiences. Even depressions, nervous breakdowns, and a "dark night of the soul" can prime the psyche for transformative resolutions of lasting power. All are means by which consciousness traverses beyond the normal, culturally-conditioned boundaries and into extreme states of the psyche for exploration and elaboration.

From these deep reserves spring the ever-refreshing waters of myth. If society's "heap of broken images" were like salvaged bricks which one could use to build new structures, then here we come upon the original brick forge itself. The task is no longer to rework or rearrange, but to *create*. The goal is to generate entirely new mythical dynamics and symbolic forms through creative myth.

LETTING PSYCHE SPEAK

One method creative mythmakers, including Jung, have used to forge a fruitful link with the unconscious is by entering into discourse with distinct mythic personalities in their own unconscious. Letting your own psyche speak in its native voices can be a crucial bridge from your own inner dynamics and the dynamics playing themselves out in other psyches the world over. Despite the seeming uniformity of our personalities—the apparently singular nature of our ego or self—such characters actually reside in *all* of us, and provide their own perspectives:

55

ones usually more in touch with the unconscious world of archetypes. It was in this way that the character of Philemon appeared to Jung and served him as a sort of guide or guru figure with whom he could converse. Much of the *Red Book* consists of dialogue in this vein. Even in his conscious life, Jung divided himself into personality No. 1 and No. 2—No. 1 being the more rational and scientific, and No. 2. the more emotive and artistic.

Such a divvying up of the psyche is not at all uncommon, especially among great minds of talent or creativity. One thinks of the composer Robert Schumann, for instance, who wrote different styles of music under different pseudonyms he'd split off from himself: Floristan and Eusebius. Similarly, the writer and philosopher Søren Kierkegaard had a whole cast of characters in his head, each with his own perspective and stage of faith. Using them, he composed his Governance-inspired. "Authorship."

Such inner personas are called "imagoes," and can serve as a significant cast of characters in our personal myth. Dan McAdams writes:

> Each of us consciously and unconsciously fashions main characters for our life stories. These characters function in our myths as if they were persons; hence, they are "personified." And each has a somewhat exaggerated and one-dimensional form; hence, they are "idealized." Our life stories may have one dominant imago or many.[2]

Such imagoes might serve as genuinely mythic personalities in our creative mythology. Indeed, the tension of their often-disparate natures and interests is itself a form of the psyche seeking resolution and a harmony of opposites. To this end, we, as mythmakers, may direct the drama, channeling psychic tension into cathartic wisdom. Larsen notes:

> In our personal mythology our story ultimately is told, and that story includes characters. The ego, I, or sense of self, whichever we choose to call it, is both immensely powerful and, at the same time, confusingly fragile. Our most important task, though, is the gaining of self-knowledge. More than merely actors, at best we are skilled directors. To put on the "good show" that comprises life we need to keep track of our inner cast.[3]

In cases like this, personal myth, self-focused, bleeds imperceptibly into creative mythology, culture-oriented. You begin down the path of personal myth by crafting a meaningful interpretation of your life experience, drawing out the inner conflicts of your psyche and personifying them, such that, through their interplay and dialogue, you begin to find catharsis and resolution. But as an expression emerging from your unconscious, your imagoes can be culturally important voices, dynamics others also feel. They may serve to populate your mythological pantheon—as daimons, perhaps, or demi- gods and goddesses, spirits, heroes or villains. As with any pantheon, the interactions between characters figures as an interplay of different fundamental forces vying for their own. Wisdom and self-knowledge lie in the harmonization of this polyphony of voices. McAdams writes:

> A personal myth may be seen as a complex set of imaginal dialogues involving different imagoes developing over narrative time.[4]

In this way, the most elementary function of personal mythmaking returns to our focus. Recall how Dan McAdams defined personal myth as, first and foremost, a story we construct "to bring together the different parts of ourselves and our lives into a purposeful and convincing whole."[5] By working with our inner cast of characters in creative mythology, we do just this, bringing into alignment not just the episodes of our experience in meaningful story, but also the different *parts* of our psyche. In the process, we also externalize common tensions others likely share. Tensions between thinking and feeling, faith and doubt, worldly cares and transcendent aspirations, etc. Within you lies a microcosm of the entire world. Name the voices and set them talking. What they work out can bring both personal resolution and cultural insight.

NEW SYMBOLS

Personal myth and creative mythology are thus, as their names suggest, shot through with paradox. Myth, something traditionally elaborated by a collective, is somehow personal; something supposedly consisting of inherent archetypes is somehow creative. The consequence, in practice, is that any individual mythmaking will necessarily exhibit both common and idiosyncratic elements. Creative myths will include both universal and unique imagery, traditional and novel, in varying degrees and dynamics.

There are many ways this can occur. We have already considered exploring your own inner psychic dimensions as mythic figures. But what about unconscious material in the deeper strata of the *collective* unconscious? There are numerous ways we might play with archetypes, and explore entirely novel configurations and dynamics between symbols for their development.

Perhaps an ancient archetype is presented through a new symbol. Or the old, traditional symbol is set in conversation with an archetype or symbol only fully developed in an unrelated tradition, thus creating a new relationship or synthesis. Or, perhaps a newly emerging archetype that has been evolving in the collective unconscious for some time is finally given a symbolic representation. Creative mythology thus emerges out of old and new elements. Creative myth, says Campbell, is that which

> springs from the unpredictable, unprecedented experience-in-illumination of an object by a subject, and the labor, then, of achieving communication of the effect. It is in this second, altogether secondary, technical phase of creative art, *communication*, that the general treasury, the dictionary so to say, of the world's infinitely rich heritage of symbols, images, myth motives, and hero deeds may be called upon... to render the message. *Or on the other hand, local, current, utterly novel themes and images may be used...* [6]

The plots of such new myths could be profound and revealing. What if Christ and Buddha were part of the same pantheon? What if God were a woman? What is the cosmological "map" of the DMT experience? The unconscious? What if angels were reincarnations? What if the Devil were redeemed back into Heaven?

Always ask, How do the old symbols speak to today? How do they seek to be transformed? Perhaps you write your own Gospel, or walk with God in the Garden. Campbell writes:

> One way to activate the imagination is to propose to it a mythic image for contemplation and free development. Mythic images—from the Christian tradition, or from any

other, for that matter, since they are all actually related—speak to very deep centers of the psyche. They came forth from the psyche originally and speak back to it. If you take in some traditional image proposed to you by your own religious tradition, your own society's religious lore, proposing it to yourself for active imagination, without any strict game rules defining the sort of thoughts you must bear in mind in relation to it... letting your own psyche enjoy and develop it, you may find yourself running into imageries, experiences, and amplifications that do not fit exactly into the patterns of the tradition in which you have been trained.[7]

Otherwise, *entirely new* images and figures can be employed to express the numinous. Perhaps these come from dreams, intuitions, visions, or any of the number of "core experiences" mentioned earlier. Here your own, idiosyncratic experience with the unconscious comes into play. Perhaps you imagine a new conception of heavenly beings, a novel rendition of angels/devas called *junnas*. Or you mythologize the magical process by which plants grow—a force you call *Elwis*, alive in all things. Or you relate the wisdom of your guardian spirit, Bemniah. Or you write a drama about the passage of a soul from one body to the next, describing all the spiritual functionaries it meets in-between. Or you compose the Ultimate Mystery as a symphony of strings. Or paint your own soul. The world of myth is open to explore.

One of the most enduring examples of creative mythology at this level of originality is the work of poet and artist William Blake (1757–1827). Blake was a visionary in every sense of the word, possessed of daringly innovative ideas as well as a profound sensitivity for channeling unconscious material. A critic of conventional organized religion, he was committed to forging his own spiritual canon of inspired works rooted in his own experience. "As he developed his personal myth," writes Leo Damrosch in his book *Eternity's Sunrise: The Imaginative World of William Blake*, "it grew challengingly complicated and increasingly strange."[8] Eventually, though, a basic story is gleaned: Albion, the primordial man, has fallen asleep, and in becoming unconscious has lost his primeval wholeness. He fragments into four personalities, or *Zoas*. These are: Urizen, who represents rationalistic thinking and the oppressive imposition of law; Luvah, the nonrational emotions; Tharmas, the unifying power; and Urthona, the creative imagination.

Los (the name of Urthona in his fallen state) is the true hero of Blake's myth. He is the craftsman, the forger, the creator, ever laboring at his smithy and challenging the relentlessly-codifying Urizen with revolutionary new forms. He labors at constructing a vast structure, the great art city of Golgonooza: a vast temple to the creative imagination. Like Albion, and the other Zoas in turn, Los also has a fragmented personality: a female emanation, Enitharmon, and a shadowy Spectre. Bringing all together in harmonious synthesis, he builds the great city of his imagination:

Therefore Los stands in London building Golgonooza,
Compelling his Spectre to labours mighty. Trembling in fear,
The Spectre weeps, but Los unmoved by tears or threats remains.
"I must create a system, or be enslaved by another man's;
I will not reason and compare: my business is to create."

So did Blake see his mythopoeic project: to create his own system, or else be fated to conform to one imposed upon him.

The system he creates is—true to the call of personal mythmaking—an expression of his own inner psychological workings. Many have noted the parallels between his inner cast of characters and those of the human psyche. Indeed, though some have been tempted to bring in Freud, Damrosch insightfully notes:

> More congenial to Blake's conception than Freud's is Jung's, which is not surprising, since Jung was interested in many of the same sources that Blake drew on. The Jungian category of thinking could be said to correspond to Urizen, intuition to Urthona, emotion to Luvah, and sense perception to Tharmas.[9]

In this way, one sees a clear connection between Blake's imagoes and Jung's psychological types. More than that, the number four (the quaternity) was the symbol of psychic wholeness in Jung's thought. (Jung, for his own part, built the Tower into four separate structures to represent this.) The Four Zoas of Albion's psychic wholeness seem reminiscent of the same idea, while the presence of a feminine subpersonality and a shadowy double are all shockingly similar to Jung's theories of the anima and shadow.

(Pages from Blake's *Jerusalem: The Emanation of the Giant Albion*)

Clearly, Blake's work taps into deep archetypal patterns. While boldly innovative, it is also elementary at the same time, reflecting in novel forms the ancient outlines of the human unconscious. In this way, he can invent from his imagination a veritable pantheon of deity-like forces in a creative epic—and yet, all the while, remain true to experience and the deep realities beyond our ken. Such is the nature of effective creative myth.

Because symbols are the language of the unconscious, to question the "veracity" or "truth-value" of such symbols is to miss the point. Myth speaks to the inner, psychic world of mankind, not the outer, objective world. As such, what matters is whether energies are activated or not, whether the new symbol is working to evoke the sense of the numinous, whether a given image works. If it does, it has something to say, something to teach us. If not, keep working with it, or try something else. Creative mythmaking is, like all creative work, an experimental process. The difference is that here, aesthetic interest is not the main goal, but rather numinous connection.

The Ultimate Mystery is just that—a profound and incomprehensible Mystery. Symbols can help to mediate our experience of it, but must never be taken as *the thing itself*. As the Buddhist expression goes, *The finger pointing at the moon is not the moon*. Symbols are tools for meditation, a means to approach the numinous. Engaging them creatively helps keep you in proper relationship to them. It is much harder to make an idol out of an image you yourself have crafted.

The threat to myth is always its turning to stone, its ossification, its concretization. This happens when one takes a symbol *literally*. It is thus objectified, and so you lose the dynamic play-exchange between the subjective and objective mindsets. The energy stops flowing, and living myth dies. Ultimately, the waste land we inhabit today came into being precisely because of this over-objectification of the world. We learned to think scientifically, and either lost or threw away our ability to think mythically.

This does not need to be the case. Science and myth can live together. Indeed, they *must*. Science has provided us an entirely new model of the universe. Psychologically, our image of the universe demands mythic expression, mythic integration. The objective world, too, must ultimately find a home in subjective mythic forms. Today, this great task likewise falls to the individual mythmaker as well. And so it is that this, too, provides a basis of material for the creative mythmaking—indeed, an urgent and important one.

A NEW COSMOS

Human beings have never stopped asking the perennial questions: Where did we come from? What are we made of? What is the shape and makeup of the universe? Such questions fill us with wonder, while their answers provide us a crucial sense of orientation.

These types of questions once found answers through myth. Today, we get them through science. Science has revealed to us the amazing grandeur of the skies and the unfathomable depths of the atom. It has told us our origins, and has provided an awesome map of our place in existence. Such things truly are the stuff of the tremendous and fascinating Ultimate Mystery. Campbell writes:

Not the neolithic peasant looking skyward with his hoe, not the old Sumerian priesthood watching planetary courses from the galleries of ziggurats, nor the modern clergyman quoting from a revised version of their book, but our own incredibly wonderful scientists today are the ones to teach us how to see: and if wonder and humility are the best vehicles to bear the soul to its hearth, I should think that a quiet Sunday morning spent at home in controlled meditation on a picture book of the galaxies might be an auspicious start for a voyage.[10]

Unfortunately, the incredible glories of our world revealed by science have not yet been *meaningfully* integrated into the collective psyche. Indeed, for many people, the new vision of the universe is mainly that of a vast, careless void, which came into being by chance and goes onward without reason or purpose to direct it. They feel today more or less as Blaise Pascal did when the implications of the new scientific discoveries were just beginning to sink in:

> When I consider the short duration of my life, swallowed up in an eternity before and after, the little space I fill engulfed in the infinite immensity of spaces whereof I know nothing, and which know nothing of me, I am terrified. The eternal silence of these infinite spaces frightens me.

Experienced in this way, the universe is only terrible, and life within it, but "a tale / Told by an idiot, full of sound and fury, / Signifying nothing." It is, in short, *meaningless.*

This does not need to be the case. The reason for this unfortunate prevalence of despair stems from the fact that our new understanding of the universe has not been meaningfully integrated into our collective consciousness. That is to say, it has not yet been *rendered mythologically*.

Science is a powerful method for understanding objective reality. Indeed, it is by far the most powerful tool ever devised by mankind for this end. What it is *not* good at is communicating that reality in ways that speak to our subjective experience, that render those truths into something emotionally and psychologically significant. This is what *myth* does.

Psychologically, humans crave *story*. We connect with narrative structures, with clear meanings and morals, and the beauty of a compelling tale well-told. This is why, for millennia, people turned to their mythic stories for satisfying answers to life's profound questions. Science, by contrast, is not interested in such things. It dwells in questions, not answers, and its focus is objective fact, without regard for how these facts are emotionally or psychologically integrated into a subjective psyche.

The result is that, today, we have a great many facts about the universe but no meaningful *story* of it. As yet, our new model of the cosmos has not found any definitive expression in the mythic modality. So long as this is the case, people will continue to experience the universe as meaningless. Because such a perspective is psychologically so taxing and emotionally unfulfilling, it is understandable why many continue to hold on to entirely outmoded mythic systems. A world made in six days, talking snakes, a boat holding all the world's animals. These are symbolically-rich myths; but, at the level of explanation for objective realities, are no more than fairy-tales. Still, even intelligent people will maintain them as literal truths if it means avoiding the only alternative: a set of facts detailing a bleak, careless universe, undirected, stretching shudderingly into a yawning infinity. A silly myth is better than a convincing chaos.

Clearly, what is desperately needed today is an account of the universe that is both in accord with our scientific understanding of it and also psychologically fulfilling. That is, we need a new mythological rendering of the cosmos, one that is right both objectively *and* subjectively. As ever, this is the task for poets and artists, not scientists, for it must speak to the heart, not just the head. It must be beautiful, not simply *correct*. As such, it is the endeavor of personal mythmaking—one of finding a new, mythic language for creation.

Fortunately, the subject matter doesn't disappoint. Its majesty and sublime scale beg to be rendered mythically. In the heavens, sprawling purple clouds that span for eons give birth to stars. Their vast explosions sow the cosmos with elemental seeds. Life emerges in the depths. Epochs of magic metamorphosis change fish to birds. A mystical code in every cell unfolds its intricate design. Consciousness emerges from the dark—to learn, to love, to create.

Here, the task is not so much the crafting of new symbols, since the subject matter is physical and not metaphysical, immanent reality and not transcendent archetypes. What we need, rather, is a new narrative, a new *Genesis*. A shared mythic telling that relates the physical processes *as* sacred history. Our culture lacks a creation myth about the Ultimate Mystery. We do not lack a Story, only its proper telling. We do not lack a great cosmological myth—only mythmakers.

For those who take up the call of creative mythology, an epic awaits to be told. Ironically, it is far grander and more sublime than we could ever have imagined. Science has revealed to us a universe of incomprehensible glory and splendor. It falls to us to lift this from the dry prose of textbooks into the solemn grandeur of poetic myth. Our greatest story has yet to be told. To do so is not just the most auspicious task for artists of any generation. It is also a service to humanity—to call people back to inhabit their world *as it is*. To help them feel at home in the universe again. And so, to return a sense of *meaning* to existence, sacralizing the heavens once more and returning to Earth its proper sense of sacredness.

Doing so would free people at last to leave behind their childish creation tales for something both grander and truer. More than that, it would dissipate the lies allowing so many to desecrate and destroy the Earth. A resacralized universe is one to be revered, not raped for raw materials. A New Myth is possible—one with new heavens and a new Earth, pervaded by the glory of the *mysterium tremendum et fascinans*.

In this way, through personal myth, the **cosmological function** of myth could be fulfilled: *to present a total image of the universe through which the ultimate mystery manifests*. We only await the poets to come who will commit themselves to the task. The personal mythmaker is called, ultimately, to communicate the universe and transform the world—a much broader and bigger calling than has hitherto been imaged for such work. But so it is. Personal mythmaking is the key to bringing meaning back into the world. It begins with the individual, but very quickly expands, for those who feel so called, into the social realm—to articulate new, living mythic symbols and even a meaningful vision of the cosmos.

However, to do so, personal myth must move beyond an individual subjective consciousness and out into the collective consciousness. That is, it must become *objective*, and so externalized. Thus we come to a crossroads. How deep are you to go with this mythmaking process? How driven are you to explore the possibilities of personal myth and your own potential for self-actualization? How far do you feel called—or fated—down the path of individuation, of carving out your own unique expressions of archetypal forms? Have you had a numinous experience? The sense of the Great Mystery "sweeping like a gentle tide, pervading the mind with a tranquil mood of deepest worship," or perhaps a "sudden eruption up from the depths of the soul" more like Jung's? Are these the secret gems of a secret personal myth, or do they call out to become something more? something you feel inspired to share with the world somehow? to work these experiences into a personal myth that's something *more than personal*—perhaps, even, a seed of the New Myth not yet on the horizon?

THE OPUS

It is one thing to maintain a personal religion as a collection of personally-meaningful symbols, ideas, memories, etc. It's a rather different thing to actually convert these from the blueprint stage in your heard to a finished building out in the world. To do this requires externalizing them into some kind of container—to craft something tangible, as Jung and Blake did, and thereby change the world.

This is truly the task of *building your cathedral.*

At a certain point, for certain people, personal myth demands outward expression. These experiences and formulations compel some kind of externalization, their making real in the world in some physical form. They long to be *communicated* to others. The communication of such myths is a key factor of Campbell's definition of creative mythology. "In what I am calling "creative" mythology," he writes, the individual has had an experience of his own—of order, horror, beauty, or even mere exhilaration—which he seeks to communicate through signs; and if his realization has been of a certain depth and import, his communication will have the value and force of living myth—for those, that is to say, who receive and respond to it themselves, with recognition, uncoerced.[11]

The precise motivation behind this urge to share will vary among individuals. It may even vary over time for the same person. Perhaps the drive is toward simple self-expression, the way the early Modernist artists sought to express themselves and their biographies through art. Or it is pure therapy, a psychiatric process for working out the unconscious stirrings within. Perhaps it is felt with all the compulsion of an exorcism—a need to purge oneself of built-up spiritual forces. Or it is experienced as prophecy: a channeling of the divine into the world for the world's edification and enlightenment. Maybe it is part of a more intentional social project, to meet the urgent demand of the world for living myth, such as the crafting of a collective cosmology. Or maybe it is entirely unclear what and why you feel the need to express such things. Perhaps you will learn what it all means afterwards, after it has been externalized and you can take it all in for what it is.

Whatever the reason behind the urge to communicate one's mythology, the project will stem from a similar origin and lead to a similar outcome in any case. You have had a meaningful insight into life, an intuition about the Ultimate Reality, and now must put it into form in order to share it with others. It must therefore take some tangible shape: book(s), painting(s), sculpture(s), song(s)—the possibilities are as endless as the media that might be used to render them.

This is called the *opus* of the creative mythmaker, and whatever form it takes, it must work to contain the mythic material and communicate it effectively to others. Bond writes: "The work, the opus, the labor provides a form that holds inner and outer experience together in the vessel of meaning."[12] Through the opus, the creative mythologist converts their individual experiences of the Ultimate Mystery into a coherent container of psychic power. It does this by translating the experience into a language that best communicates the ineffable qualities of the numinous experience into images and symbols.

Like all inspiration, the original experience may have been immediate and passively received, but the translation process itself is a reflective, conscious activity. Indeed, it may be long and arduous, with many fits and starts, just to communicate. This period can be immensely fruitful for the mythmaker, as an opportunity to further clarify and flesh out what in the "blueprint" phase remained hazy and uncertain. Ultimately, says Bond, "the cultural form that the myth takes requires a conscious labor, an opus, but the vision itself is a product of psyche."[13] Whoever would seek to do this must become an *artist* of their myth.

Regardless of what else such creations might be, there is an undeniable link between this process and the work of the *artist*. Simply put, the external formation of non-traditional, personally-resonant mythic imagery is an imaginative aesthetic enterprise. The inner voice in Jung's head recognized this even before he did. To fashion a creative myth is to make a work of art of some kind or another.

Art, of course, is hard to define and pin down. Things can be art even while serving other, perhaps more primary functions. In fact, most of the pictorial "art" from history, so-called, was originally engaged religiously, as objects for meditation and religious contemplation. What one person sees as a work of art might, for another person, be seen as a religious icon. Neither are wrong. Jung saw what he was doing as something other than art. That does not stop millions of people from admiring his *Red Book* as an aesthetic object.

The relationship between art and religious material culture is rich and deep, and goes back to the dawn of time. Cave paintings, the very first examples of art we know of, are believed to have been primarily used for magical and shamanistic purposes. The first poets told mythic stories of gods and spirits; prophecy itself was poetry, and poetry prophecy. The very word "inspiration" (the process of being inhabited or influenced by spiritual forces) still relates to both religious authority (an "inspired" scripture) and aesthetic artfulness and ingenuity (an "inspired" work). Art and mythmaking are intricately bound, and always have been.

Indeed, Campbell has suggested that the artist and the mystic share a fundamental orientation to the world. The very "yes" we say to our life and consequently the world is, he claims, the same "yes" to life that inspires the artist to create. For Campbell, the true artist is neither teacher nor activist, neither provocateur nor marketer; the true artist is pushing nothing—only presenting the world *as it is* in an expression of that pure inner gratitude for being. Thus "the first function of art is exactly that which I have already named as the first function of mythology..."[14] The artist performs the metaphysical function of myth. In this way, the true artist is, fundamentally, a mystic.

In a world now devoid of religious seers, shamans, and prophets, it falls upon the mythic artist to continue the mystical function of mythmaking in the world. This they do by translating their personal experience of the holy into outward symbols that can serve as evocations and suggestions to others for how *they* can experience the holy for themselves. They play the midwife to others' spiritual development, working by indirect means to ignite a subjective connection with the Source. Campbell writes:

> we move—each—in two worlds: the inward of our own awareness, and an outward of participation in the history of our time and place. ...Creative artists...are mankind's awakeners to recollection: summoners of our outward mind to conscious contact with ourselves, not as participants in this or that morsel of history, but as spirit, in the consciousness of being. Their task, therefore, is to communicate directly from one inward world to another, in such a way that an actual shock of experience will have been rendered: not a mere statement for the information or persuasion of the brain, but an effective communication across the void of space and time from one center of consciousness to another. ... *The mythogenetic zone today is in the individual in contact with his own interior life, communicating through his art with those "out there."*[15]

Creative mythology thus entails more than simply "getting the point across" about a numinous or sacred experience. It is more than a recounting of an event or an essayistic description of what you think it all means. Rather, creative mythology is *evocative*—it *calls out* something from within the audience. It employs the imagistic language of symbols to work on the inner worlds of the audience to help facilitate their own wonder and to inspire their own imaginations. It does this, Jung might say, by activating the archetypes latent in the audience, and thus arousing their own organic response of mystery and wonder.

Creative mythologies thus aspire to the same sort of reception that religious myth and ritual sought to evoke, but no longer can. But what is dead in the traditions can emerge with all vitality in the living myths of today's creative mythologists. No doubt there are still many people who, when opening the Bible, are filled with excitement and a sense of wonder before a sacred, numinous text. However, such an experience is becoming less and less common as the symbols therein and the mythic system they inform lose their grip on the imagination. They are more likely to be encountered as old, overly familiar, outdated, dead. Opening the *Red Book*, however, or an illuminated copy of Blake's *Jerusalem*, is a very different experience. You immediately feel an electric pulse, of wonder and uncertainty, interest and curiosity. Indeed, you feel the tug of the *mysterium tremendum et fascinans*. Here is living water. Not necessarily because it is more *true* than ancient Scripture, but only because the symbols are still speaking, still dynamic, still vital. Here, one feels, is a genuine personal encounter with the Source, whatever that may mean. As such, it is compelling, fascinating, captivating. It activates the archetypal energies in a way old systems no longer can.

Whatever the specific driving motivation for the mythologist to create, this is ultimately the end one strives toward. Creative myth causes living water to flow once more in our spiritual desert. For those receptive to it, it opens a portal to the deep unconscious Source of myth, which, in religious traditions—now dead and ossified—had remained barred. This is the meaningful vocation of the creative mythmaker.

MYTHS OF PURPOSE, PURPOSE IN MYTH

Such tasks are clearly of great importance—especially today, when meaning is so desperately sought, but direction so unclear. The influence of the contemporary mythmaker, then, could not be overstated. Their work can and will literally change the world.

And so it is that personal mythmaking of the most elementary kind discussed at the outset loops back to such high-flown creative mythmaking which includes the crafting of artistic mythologies for the world. That is, for some, the communication of mythic images becomes for them a goal of immense personal importance. For such people, the commitment to the project of crafting and sharing their creative myth is itself the anchor of their life story—the imaginative act that frames their life as an integrated and purposeful whole. Communicating their personal experience of the sacred becomes the driving motivator of their personal narrative. *What is my meaning? To make myths and share them.* One's personal myth is being a creative myth-maker.

Our horizons tell our story, and presently they are full of shallow monuments to only our baser drives and of empty of all meaningful endeavor. Though the skylines rise with soaring peaks, we live in a spiritual desert, a barren wasteland stretching forward without interruption. To replenish that desert, to fill the world again with myth, to activate in others the sense of meaning and wonder—this, surely, is a worthy task. Here we spiral back to the psychological function of myth: producing the New Myth is indeed a thing to live for, a mythic seizure, something to motivate us—not just for ourselves, but for the world in which we live. In this way, personal myth ties us back to our broader context, to fulfill the psychological function of myth in its most robust expression:

75

the centering and unfolding of the individual in integrity, in accord with himself (the microcosm), culture (the mesocosm), the universe (the macrocosm), and that awesome ultimate mystery which is both beyond and within himself and all things.[16]

Such is the calling of contemporary mythmaking, which strives, ultimately, toward that New Myth beyond the horizon, the one that will renew people's sense of meaning and place, the one that will gather them together in shared aspiration, the one that will motivate a new and renewed civilization.

MASTER PLAN

A SHARED DREAM

Ultimately, we can see that the term "personal myth" is a bit misleading. For while it is indeed something we construct by ourselves, its impacts can nevertheless be felt *far* beyond us.

A functioning personal myth is a life-changing story—at any level. It can take a person from depression and despair to wholeness and meaning. Even such personal transformations are not without far-reaching external consequences. They affect the environments in which those people live. Our orientation to life is felt by others. As McAdams notes,

> The stories we create influence the stories of other people, those stories give rise to still others, and soon we find meaning and connection within a web of story making and story living. Through our personal myths, we help to create the world we live in, at the same time that it is creating us.[1]

As the meaning crisis continues to expand, such a positive influence is needed now more than ever. Personal myth changes the world from the inside out.

The impact is even bigger when one has heeded the call to *externalize* their personal myths in an opus for sharing with the world. Today, in the breakdown of the old religious systems, these creative myths become like small lights in a dimming world. Indeed, they might be someone's *only* genuine engagement with living myth! Around these tiny fires we huddle.

But, couldn't they also serve to re-ignite the flame of myth in our society?

Jung saw the source of every society's renewal in *individuals*, whenever they navigate beyond the walls of their culture and bring back to it some novel insight for the collective's development. This is what individuation is all about. The expansion of consciousness transforms the individual, but also has the potential to transform *their culture* as well. However, this can only happen if their insights are able to find a way to become successfully *integrated* into the culture. If they can, the entire scope of cultural consciousness expands, bringing new insights, new directions, new possibilities for the group. Culture is renewed.

In his book *Living Myth*, D. Stephenson Bond sees personal myth as the key vehicle for this expansion of cultural consciousness at a time when we lack a shared, living myth. He writes:

> When a culture has reached its limit, the development of culture must paradoxically come from outside of culture. How is a culture to renew itself except through individuals who restore the cultural imagination? That is, *where do the sustaining myths of culture come but from what were once personal myths in individual lives?*[2]

The decline of traditional religions has placed the burden of crafting a meaningful life onto the individual. But this does not mean that meaning must be only personal from now on. The task has fallen to individuals to craft meaningful myths out of their experience, but, once crafted, these myths can be *put back* into culture—through the diffusion of creative mythologies.

Every new opus adds new possibilities to reactivate the latent archetypes within each member of society. Indeed, every new opus provides another example to others of what myth is and how it works, and what *personal* myth is and how it works. Every opus thus renders its meaning-making goal that much more legitimate and feasible in the eyes of society. In all of these ways, creative mythology kindles the imagination of others—rekindles the mythic imagination of the group. Thus, as Bond says, "the birth of the personal myth in the imagination of a single individual may become the rebirth of the greater myths in the imagination of the culture."[3]

What if we cultivated intentional communities specifically devoted to this task? Communities dedicated to the crafting of personal myths, and sustaining the invitational and open space to share them? Where people could come to write, draw, paint, compose, etc., in the context of a shared mission?

At present, such communities are rare, but some do exist. A notable example is *CoSM*, a community in Wappinger Falls, New York, founded by visionary artists Alex and Allyson Grey. There, in a stately house on 40 wooded acres, "Art Church" services are held, inviting people to come and express their inner divinity through art. "Each of us carry a spark of the Almighty Force of the Universe," the Greys write,

> that seeks expression through our lives and works. We gather as community to activate our creativity as spiritual practice. The Universal Creative Force is the Divine Artist and Cosmos is the evolving masterwork of Creation. When we make art together, a new way of seeing may emerge. As Sacred Mirrors, we reflect and re-inforce the redemptive transformative power of art in each of our lives.[4]

What if "church" more and more became such an "art church"? A community of support for expressing the divine in all of us through creative mythmaking? Here communal ritual enters in—not as a magical act to propitiate a deity, but as a shared containing space for incubating personal intimations of the divine and externalizing them through art.

Such is the driving motivation behind so-called "visionary art." In his book *The Mission of Art*, Alex Grey writes:

> The visionary artist may inwardly apprehend, then uniquely transmit traditional sacred archetypes or create previously undisclosed forms, beings, and vistas. The covenant that visionary art makes with a viewer is to catalyze the viewer's own deepest insight by plunging them headlong into the symbolic mystery play of life, planting seeds for their future spiritual unfoldment.[5]

Through art, the collective consciousness is expanded. Perhaps, had Jung listened to the voice in his head that said "It is art," he might have gone in just this sort of direction. In any event, personal myth is an artistic production. Grey embraces this idea, and sees this as the means by which the divine is communicated and developed:

> God has ordained that imagination be stronger than reason in the soul of the artist, which makes the artist build bridges between the possible and seemingly impossible. How do artists gain insight into their own character and realize their own unique vision? By entering the studio in your heart, all artists have access to a personal yet universal vision that can guide and inspire them and, perhaps, all of us.[6]

In the past, personal visions were always deemed a threat to the official religious authority. Doctrines and creeds needed to be maintained; orthodoxy was everything. The idea that people could fashion their own personal images of the divine, letting themselves be inspired by a multitude of mythic symbols for their own unique transformations and even creating their own was anathema. It was, indeed, "heresy," a word that meant "choice." Choice and creativity were the last thing official churches could tolerate. Personal visions were thus largely denigrated and suppressed.

Today, however, religious authorities are no longer in a position to do this. Incredible freedom now exists, which we must put to better use than apathy and nihilism. Unfortunately, the same objective rationalism that pushed back the power of religious authorities now keeps the people stuck in its own tyranny of materialism. The pendulum has swung the other way.

Slowly, we are finding our way through the maze. At last, the task has become clarified; the way lies before us: to make use of our hard-won spiritual freedom by putting it into the service of shaping the New Myth. This is the task that history now demands of us—the task of *creative spirituality*.

A TEMPLE OF VAST DIMENSIONS

Our personal myths, then, are not so personal after all. They have the potential to affect society for the better, and in the most crucial way. In a civilization that has lost its myth—and thus its aspiration, its great purpose—single individuals, expressing their mythic imaginations, can help *restore* the mythic sensibility and shape the *new mythology* for our time.

In the enveloping darkness of our modern world, each personal myth provides another candle of illumination. Indeed, they have been working "in the dark," so to speak, for some time—quietly but steadily laying a new foundation for the modern spirit. As Bond powerfully expresses it:

> the long and lonely labor, the fears and doubts and countless failures that the evolution of a personal myth claims in the life of a single individual, are endured not only for self, but for others as well. I do not think it is possible to realize just how large an unconscious foundation for a newly evolving myth may already have been built on our behalf, though unacknowledged and as yet undiscovered.[7]

Our personal myths have been laying the groundwork for the coming collective myth, acknowledged or not. In this way, the "cathedrals" of our personal myths are, like Jung's Tower, only part of something much, *much* bigger: a vast complex of rising mythic structures, all assembled independently and yet *working together* to form one harmonious whole. This is the true Cathedral: the coming Myth, on which we all build.

Jung had a sense of this vast, ongoing project in the collective unconscious. Edward Edinger relates a fascinating exchange in his book *The Creation of Consciousness: Jung's Myth for Modern Man*. He recounts there how a Jungian analyst once had the following dream:

> *A temple of vast dimensions was in the process of being built. As far as I could see—ahead, behind, right and left—there were incredible numbers of people building on gigantic pillars. I, too, was building on a pillar. The whole building process was in its very beginning, but the foundations were already there, the*

rest of the building was starting to go up, and I and many others were working on it.

When Jung was told about this dream, Edinger says, he knowingly replied:

> Yes, you know, that is the temple we all build on. We don't know the people because, believe me, they build in India and China and in Russia and all over the world. That is the new religion. You know how long it will take until it is built? . . . about six hundred years.[8]

THE UNCONSCIOUS MYTH

It was Jung, of course, who recognized that people's dreams can spring from either their own personal unconscious or from the collective unconscious. In these latter, "big" dreams, one can get a glimpse of what huge, tectonic shifts are occurring beneath the surface of humanity's psyche. They reveal what is still gestating inside us, waiting to be born. The analyst's dream described above was just such a dream.

Appreciating this, we can see how this dream is actually not unique, but one in a *constellation* of similar dreams whose images and ideas have been simmering below for some time, in psyches the world over. For example, Bond relates this remarkable dream of a male patient of his:

> *I am in the vast reaches of interstellar space. No sun, no earth, no sound, only the silent starts all around. I'm walking along a thin line of liquid fire, maybe two feet wide. The fire burns intensely, but doesn't hurt me and is solid to walk on. I'm*

thinking as I walk, "This is familiar. I know what this is . . .," like those times when there's a word just on the tip of your tongue. You know you know it. So the issue in the dream is recognition. Will I recognize what this fiery red line that is so familiar to me truly is? Suddenly I'm lifted up above the line to a much higher point of view. Now I see that my one red line that I was walking is but one of many lines. Other lines connect and intersect with my line. In fact, as I get higher still I see that all of the lines are connected in a vastly complicated beautiful living circle burning in space. My line is now one line among many in a great pattern that connects each in a subtle harmony. I see that I have been walking toward the center of the circle. Then I have the recognition I have been seeking. I realize, "This is my life." That is why it was so absolutely familiar to me.[9]

In this revelatory dream, it is the life of the man—his life story, his narrative, his personal myth—that he follows like a path of destiny. It leads ultimately to a vast cosmic web of other such lives, all interweaving and working together to form a much greater Whole: "a vastly complicated beautiful living circle burning in space." But... what is this?

Myths relate the *numinous* through the language of symbol. It is through myth that we communicate the Ultimate Mystery, the *mysterium tremendum et fascinans*. A New Myth means a new expression of the *numinous* Reality. A New Myth, operating at the level of a new religion, means a new relationship between the collective and the sacred. Lived out, internalized, meditated upon, a New Myth means a new understanding of God—a new "God-image." The development of a New Myth, then, means the development of a new conception of God.

It is this that we see symbolically expressed in the collective unconscious. The New Myth is taking shape, and with it, a new God-image. Indeed, the two are intricately related. For *the New Myth is itself about mankind's role in shaping the divine.* Through its own conscious development, humanity aids in the transformation of the divine.

Jung, too, had the dream rocking the collective unconscious of mankind. More than any other, probably, he helped bring it to conscious awareness. In doing so, he found not only his personal myth, but the myth in which *all* our personal myths play their God-shaping part. It occurred to him at last during a series of travels to New Mexico and the African savannah.

In 1925, still in the midst of composing the *Red Book*, Jung visited the Pueblo Indians in New Mexico, and asked some of them about their religious beliefs and practices, whereupon he learned about their rituals of assisting the sun every day in its travels across the sky. "The Americans want to stamp out our religion," said Mountain Lake, chief of the Taos pueblos, to Jung.

"Why can they not let us alone? What we do, we do not only for ourselves but for the Americans also. Yes, we do it for the whole world. Everyone benefits by it."
I could observe from his excitement that he was alluding to some extremely important element of his religion. I therefore asked him: "You think, then, that what you do in your religion benefits the whole world?" He replied with great animation. "Of course. If we did not do it, what would become of the world?" And with a significant gesture he pointed to the sun. I felt that we were approaching extremely delicate ground here, verging on the mysteries of the tribe. "After all," he said, "we are a people who live on the roof of the world; we

85

are the sons of the Father Sun, and with our religion we daily help our father to go across the sky. We do this not only for ourselves, but for the whole world. If we were to cease practising our religion, in ten years time the sun would no longer rise. Then it would be night forever."[10]

With this, Jung appreciated for the first time what it truly means to live mythologically, to have a myth of true cosmic importance. The division between such an existence and the relative insignificance of one lived purely within the objective rationalism of the modern world was painfully clear to him. Regarding his Indian interlocutor, Jung saw,

> his life is cosmologically meaningful, for he helps the father and preserver of all life in his daily rise and descent. If we set against this our own self-justifications, the meaning of our own lives as it is formulated by our reason, we cannot help but see our poverty. Out of sheer envy we are obliged to smile at the Indians' naiveté and to plume ourselves on our cleverness; for otherwise we would discover how impoverished and down at the heels we are.[11]

Specifically, what we lack through our modern perspective is any sense of having an *impact on the transcendent realm*. Nothing we do affects God; we have nothing to offer the Ultimate Mystery. According to the man of science, our lives are just specks in space; to the man of myth, though, our lives are part of a divine drama, in which we aid the deity in performing its crucial, life-giving acts. But what would a new such myth look like? What would it mean for human lives to be of cosmic significance today?

Jung received an answer to this most pivotal question on the savannah plains of Africa. There he had something akin to an experience of primeval awareness—of feeling like the first consciousness to gaze out on the world and so instantiate it. "From a low hill in this broad savanna," he writes,

> a magnificent prospect opened out to us. To the very brink of the horizon we saw gigantic herds of animals: gazelle, antelope, gnu, zebra, warthog, and so on. Grazing, heads nodding, the herds moved forward like slow rivers. There was scarcely any sound save the melancholy cry of a bird of prey. This was the stillness of the eternal beginning, the world as it had always been, in the state of non-being; for until then no one had been present to know that it was this world. I walked away from my companions until I had put them out of sight, and savored the feeling of being entirely alone. There I was now, the first human being to recognize that this was the world, but who did not know that in this moment he had first really created it. There the cosmic meaning of consciousness became overwhelmingly clear to me. ... My old Pueblo friend [Mountain Lake] came to my mind. He thought that the *raison d'etre* of his pueblo had been to help their father, the sun, to cross the sky each day. I had envied him for the fullness of meaning in that belief, and had been looking about without hope for a myth of our own. Now I knew what it was, and knew even more: that man is indispensable for the completion of creation; that, in fact, he himself is the second creator of the world, who alone has given to the world its objective existence without which, unheard, unseen, silently eating, giving birth, dying, heads nodding through hundreds of millions of years, it would have gone on in the profoundest

night of non-being down to its unknown end. Human consciousness created objective existence and meaning, and man found his indispensable place in the great process of being.[12]

By becoming *conscious* of the world, humans "bring it into being," so to speak. Our consciousness is needed to raise the world out of the unconscious and into the light of phenomenal reality. We did not cause the universe to exist; but without us, the universe would never be conscious.

And, indeed, thought Jung, it was precisely toward this consciousness that all of history and evolution have been tending. "Natural history," he writes,

> tells us of a haphazard and casual transformation of species over hundreds of millions of years of devouring and being devoured. The biological and political history of man is an elaborate repetition of the same thing. But the history of the mind offers a different picture. Here the miracle of reflection consciousness intervenes—the second cosmogony. The importance of consciousness is so great that one cannot help suspecting the element of *meaning* to be concealed somewhere within all the monstrous, apparently senseless biological turmoil, and that the road to its manifestation was ultimately found on the level of warm-blooded vertebrates possessed of a differentiated brain—found as if by chance, unintended and unforeseen, and yet somehow sensed, felt and groped for out of some dark urge.[13]

The universe had been in a state of unconsciousness for billions of years. Eventually, creatures arose who rendered it, to greater or lesser degrees, conscious. But it is not done. *More* still must be brought out of the unconscious and into consciousness. What, exactly?

God.

Deep within, still unconscious, God is there. Every time we reconnect with our unconscious and bring forth material we externalize into myth, we are bringing God to greater conscious awareness—to others' awareness, and *to this emerging God's own Self-awareness.* "That is the meaning of divine service," writes Jung,

> of the service which man can render to God, that light may emerge from the darkness, that the Creator may become conscious of his creation, and man conscious of himself. That is the goal, or one goal, which fits man meaningfully into the scheme of creation, and at the same time confers meaning upon it. It is an explanatory myth which has slowly taken shape within me in the course of the decades.[14]

By exploring his unconscious and rendering it in material form for conscious reflection, Jung had fulfilled his "task of tasks" and uncovered his own personal myth. As it turns out, though, to craft a personal myth is to partake in a much larger mythic endeavor. To give expression to your own sense of the *numinous* is to participate in the *Numinous* coming further into consciousness, to the Ultimate Mystery becoming known. Giving shape to your God-image contributes to the overall development of the God-image. In telling your story, you add a piece to the cosmic Story. We are all working on The Cathedral.

LINES CONVERGING:
THE MYTH OF MYTHMAKING

This process has been going on for millennia. Indeed, every religion at every stage of its development has been engaged in this task of tasks, in building The Cathedral. As new stages in development are reached, old symbols lose their efficacy and new symbols appear. New sections of The Cathedral are worked at. Now it is sacrifice, now mastery of desire, now law, now forgiveness, now love—and so forth. The myths shift through the ages, until... the myth itself becomes *the myth of God's transformation*.

By means of this process, the God slumbering in the unconscious grows more and more awake. Albion stirs. Edinger expresses the New Myth in his own mythic image this way:

Suppose the universe consists of an omniscient mind containing total and absolute knowledge. But it is asleep. Slowly it stirs, stretches and starts to awaken. It begins to ask questions. What am I? — but no answer comes. Then it thinks, I shall consult my fantasy, I shall do active imagination. With that, galaxies and solar systems spring into being. The fantasy focuses on earth. It becomes autonomous and life appears. Now the Divine mind wants dialogue and man emerges to answer that need. The deity is straining for Self-knowledge and the noblest representatives of mankind have the burden of that divine urgency imposed on them. Many are broken by the weight. A few survive and incorporate the fruits of their divine encounter in mighty works of religion and art and human knowledge. These then generate new ages and civilizations in the history of mankind. Slowly, as this process unfolds, God begins to learn who He is.[15]

This is humanity's great task of tasks—to awaken the God slumbering in our collective unconscious so that we may know God and God may know God's Self. This is the divine labor we work at. This is our version of assisting the sun transverse the sky. We do it by bringing forth the God within us by means of our personal myths. All of our efforts thus work together into one great project.

This is the New Myth still attempting to break into greater and greater consciousness. This is the significance of the symbols seething in the world's big dreams. Recall Bond's patient, who dreamed of his life's line forming the sacred geometry of the One mandala Self:

Now I see that my one red line that I was walking is but one of many lines. Other lines connect and intersect with my line. In fact, as I get higher still I see that all of the lines are connected in a vastly complicated beautiful living circle burning in space. My line is now one line among many in a great pattern that connects each in a subtle harmony. I see that I have been walking toward the center of the circle. Then I have the recognition I have been seeking. I realize, "This is my life." That is why it was so absolutely familiar to me.

Edinger relates a similar dream, recounted by a woman:

I saw the earth covered by a single great Tree whose multiple roots fed on the Inner Sun of Gold, the lumen naturae. It was a tree whose limbs were made of light and the branches were lovingly entangled so that it made itself a network of beauteous love. And it seemed as if it were lifting itself out of the broken seeds of many, countless egos who had now allowed the One Self to break forth. And when one beheld this, the sun and the moon and the planets turned out to be something quite, quite other than one had thought. From what I could make out, the Lord Himself was the Alchemist, and out of collecting swarming and suffering, ignorance and pollution, He was "trying" the gold.[16]

So the new God emerges—from the collective unconscious to the collective consciousness. But, the dream suggests, God is not passive in the process. While we add our own part into the mix, the emerging God tests our metal, "trying" the gold, passing judgment on His own taking-shape, confirming or rejecting. So it is a dialectic—humans bringing God to greater Self-consciousness, and that Self-consciousness assessing our work along the way: indeed, *using* us to bring Himself into expression.

In his book *The Varieties of Religious Experience*, William James relates a number of visionary experiences people have reported in the course of dreams, trances, hallucinations, ether intoxication, and the like. One powerful narrative struck me upon first reading the book many years ago. Now, in retrospect, I wonder if it doesn't express the same myth, simmering even then in the collective unconscious at the turn of the century. A woman relates her vision:

A great Being or Power was traveling through the sky, his foot was on a kind of lightning as a wheel is on a rail, it was his pathway. The lightning was made entirely of the spirits of innumerable people close to one another, and I was one of them. He moved in a straight line, and each part of the streak or flash came into its short conscious existence only that he might travel. I seemed to be directly under the foot of God, and I thought he was grinding his own life up out of my pain. Then I saw that what he had been trying with all his might to do was to change his course, to bend the line of lightning to which he was tied, in the direction in which he wanted to go. I felt my flexibility and helplessness, and knew that he would succeed. He bended me, turning his corner by means of my hurt, hurting me more than I had ever been hurt in my life, and at the acutest point of this, as he passed, I saw. I understood for a moment things that I have now forgotten, things that no one could remember while retaining sanity. The angle was an obtuse angle, and I remember thinking as I woke that had he made it a right or acute angle, I should have both suffered and 'seen' still more, and should probably have died.

He went on and I came to. In that moment the whole of my life passed before me, including each little meaningless piece of distress, and I understood them. This was what it had all meant, this was the piece of work it had all been contributing to do. I did not see God's purpose, I only saw his intentness and his entire relentlessness towards his means. He thought no more of me than a man thinks of hurting a cork when he is opening wine, or hurting a cartridge when he is firing. And yet, on waking, my first feeling was, and it came with tears, 'Domine non sum digna' [Lord, I am not worthy], for I had been lifted into a position for which I was too small. I realized that in that half hour under ether I had served God more distinctly and purely than I had ever done in my life before, or than I am capable of desiring to do. I was the means of his achieving and revealing something, I know not what or to whom, and that, to the exact extent of my capacity for suffering. While regaining consciousness, I wondered why, since I had gone so deep, I had seen nothing of what the saints call the love of God, nothing but his relentlessness. And then I heard an answer, which I could only just catch, saying, 'Knowledge and Love are One, and the measure is suffering.'[7]

Deep within, God is working—on His own "task of tasks," you might say, achieving His own aim relentlessly. Here it is not the dreamer riding the line of their life, but God moving, like a locomotive, along His, traveling—*by means of us*. Indeed, we ourselves come into our short consciousness only *so that* God can travel His way. In this, our lives are the means by which God works his Purpose. And, by means of certain individuals, He *changes course*—His Way is transformed. This is our divine service, the labor we lend to help God achieve His purpose. It is experienced as suffering, the depth of which measures both our love and our knowledge of the Ultimate Mystery.

OUR NEW HORIZON

Such dreams and visions are nothing less than the nascent scriptures of the New Myth on the horizon. As yet, it remains mostly underground, a subterranean theology brimming with energy beneath the threshold of consciousness. Myths such as this bring it to the surface, put it into the world, making the new God-image conscious. Ultimately, this is the task our personal myths can serve as well, as we devote our individual lives to the mythic service of the Mystery. Edinger writes:

As it gradually dawns on people, one by one, that the transformation of God is not just an interesting idea but is a living reality, it may begin to function as a new myth. Whoever recognizes this myth as his own personal reality will put his life in the service of this process.[18]

Indeed, every individual effort here is helpful. No experience is wasted. In this sense, the cultural meaning crisis can actually turn out to be a necessary and constructive process, provided that enough people work through its implications toward some personal psychological growth: the expansion and development of their God-image. In his book *The New God-Image*, Edinger writes:

If enough individuals have had that transformative experience within themselves, then they become seeds sown in the collective psyche which can promote the unification of the collective psyche as a whole. Society is no more than the sum total of all the individuals that make it up. It is not anything else. Therefore, the collective psyche of the human race is the sum total of all the individual psyches. If a certain number of individuals psyches have had the experience whereby the God-image, by reaching consciousness, has achieved the transformation, then those few individuals will function something like yeast in the dough.[19]

Bond imagines this communal construction of God rather beautifully. Writing at the end of *Living Myth*, he concludes:

The world of many generations elaborates a myth. … Line by line it slowly crystallizes. Image by image it becomes living myth. Like a temple of vast dimensions, in the early stages we do not see how the pieces fit together, because we do not know the blueprint. It is as if each life is a vehicle of crystallization in which something takes shape, something is given substance. As if an individual life is a work station, or probably just a single shift at work because our time is so limited. We take the work as far as we can take it and then hand it off to others. It is often lonely labor done in secret. In the morning we receive instruction from the night shift. They tell us how the work's progressed and try to bring us up to date on what's been done so far. As best they can, they try to tell us the task that lies before us. If they've done well, we feel a certain admiration and see clearly what is to be done next. If they faltered, we begin the day by going back and reworking the unfinished pieces. Perhaps from time to time we meet others who with different skills are working the same piece as our own. …We work our piece as skill and talent allow straight through until evening. …If we are fortunate we earn the satisfaction of a good day's labor and, retiring for the evening, catch a glimpse of the larger structure taking shape as we walk away. And then smile.[20]

This is the Cathedral we are all working on, whose foundations have already been laid by countless personal myths the world over. With every evocative new image, every compelling new form, every illuminating new symbol, we are transforming God, building God. As Jung noted, "that is the temple we all build on. We don't know the people because, believe me, they build in India and China and in Russia and all over the world. That is the new religion." And it is taking shape slowly and, still, mostly unconsciously. Indeed, making it more conscious is our first task— and this is precisely what the opus of your personal myth does— no solitary task, but the basis of what could be a global movement, a social aspiration for a world still without myth.

Campbell remarked, "The rise and fall of civilizations in the long, broad course of history can be seen to have been largely a function of the integrity and cogency of their supporting canons of myth; for not authority but *aspiration* is the motivator, builder, and transformer of civilization."[21] So, for example, the cathedrals, which united Europe at the height of an aspirational spirituality to construct something good and beautiful, together, for the future. It was a shared myth that united them in collective effort. Indeed, it was participating in that myth that excited people's imaginations toward their own collective opus. Campbell writes:

> The cathedrals, the great temples of the world, or the work of any artist who has given his life to producing these things—all of these come from mythic seizure, not from Maslow's values. That awakening of awe, that awakening of zeal, is the beginning, and, *curiously enough, that's what pulls people together.*[22]

It is the call of Purpose that unites us. Not just to bring together the disconnected fragments of our lives into a coherent whole, but to bring together each of our disconnected lives into a unifying endeavor. Personal mythmaking becomes social mythmaking. We labor to build The Cathedral *together*.

In this way, we can imagine that personal mythmaking, thus developed toward the New Myth, could also fulfill the **sociological function** of myth: namely, *to validate and maintain a certain moral order of laws for living with others in society.* The New Myth is a social myth. It calls us all to collective work. Inherent within it is an ethic rooted in the project itself. That ethic is not dogmatic in the sense of imposing a creed, but invitational in the sense of encouraging individualistic participation. It eschews strict rules, rigidity, and conformity, and welcomes playfulness, inventiveness, imagination. At the heart of everything, a profound reverence, a solemnity of calling, a sense of mission, and a worshipful appreciation for life *as it is* as a microcosmic expression of the Ultimate Reality *as it is*—the *mysterium tremendum et fascinans* that rides our life like an unstoppable locomotive and yet also depends upon us for achieving its own Self-actualization.

THE CATHEDRAL

A man dreams:

> *I have been set a task nearly too difficult for me. A log of hard and heavy wood lies covered in the forest. I must uncover it, saw or hew from it a circular piece, and then carve through the piece a design. The result is to be preserved at all costs, as representing something no longer recurring and in danger of being lost. At the same time a tape recording is to be made describing in detail what it is, what it represents, its whole meaning. At the end, the thing itself and the tape are to be given to the public library. Someone says that only the library will know how to prevent the tape from deteriorating within five years.*[23]

Our individual lives are all utterly unique, and thus precious. No one will ever have your experience, come to your realizations, encounter the unconscious in just the way you will. Your life is significant. And to the extent that you labor at some meaningful descent into the psyche to bear God back to the surface for the world to integrate, you participate in the New Myth. You build God out of your own life. The God that emerges reflects your experience, your life. In this way, your life is literally *saved*, preserved, as *part of God.*

Edinger, who relates the above dream, interprets it as an image of the New Myth. The difficult task is the individual's life—and it is to be preserved at all costs, added into a treasury that will keep it from disappearing. "The new myth postulates that no authentic consciousness achieved by the individual is lost. Each increment augments the collective treasury."[24] We all become part of the Whole. The Cathedral *is* that treasury. It is made of us.

Edinger sees this idea prefigured in various mythic images that have already come to consciousness, even if their full import has not been grasped. It is already in the Bible, for instance, in the Book of Revelation. So, at the final culmination of history, we read:

> He who is victorious—I will make him a pillar in the temple of my God; he shall never leave it. And I will write the name of my God upon him, and the name of the city of my God, that new Jerusalem which is coming down out of heaven from my God, and my own name.

In the end, we *become* the Temple. The development of the God-image in the New Myth culminates in this Temple comprised of all our individual consciousnesses—our multitude of personal myths all intersecting their lines together to form the great Circle.

The image, I think, appears likewise in Dante's *Divine Comedy*, the poet's vision of Heaven culminating in the sight of the sempiternal Celestial Rose, where all the souls of the faithful persist for eternity around the divinity. "Understood psychologically," says Edinger, such texts

> refer to a transfer or translation from the temporal, personal life of the ego to the eternal, archetypal realm. Presumably

the essential accomplishments of egohood, its final *sublimatio* in the collective, archetypal treasury of humanity. Jung seems to be saying the same thing in describing the visions he had when on the verge of death:

> I had the feeling that everything was being sloughed away....Nevertheless something remained; it was as if I now carried along with me everything I had ever experienced or done, everything that had happened around me. ...I consisted of my own history, and I felt with great certainty: this is what I am. [25]

Freed of temporal limitations, the sum of individual consciousness continues on, forever—built into the very architecture of The Cathedral of the emerging God. Towards a vision such as this the new God-image has been developing. The Great Self, a vast mandala—the symbol of psychic wholeness—made up of countless selves.

("Collective Vision" by Alex Grey)

EPILOGUE: GETTING TO WORK

We must start somewhere, though. Even for the most towering structures, we work one small piece at a time. The first is always the hardest. Ultimately, all you need is yourself to make a beginning. The New Myth, if it is to emerge, must begin with single individuals laboring at their own lives, their own direct encounters with the numinous, their own personal myths.

Personal myth opens up into the domain of something akin to a personal religion when you apply the same "Yes-saying" that you did to your life to the whole of existence. With this, you affirm the meaning of your life *as it is* within the matrix of an infinitely vaster cosmic Mystery *as it is*. This Mystery, when directly encountered as a meaningful Whole, affects a sense of awe, wonder, and gratitude. It is the Ultimate Reality that is both incomprehensible and fascinating, evoking your affirmation and assent not through reason or morality, but through sheer overwhelming grandeur.

Experiences of this sort are called numinous experiences. Though once communicated via traditional religious systems, the numinous connection with the world has dwindled as modern forces undermined religion and forced a break between objective reality and subjective experiences of meaning. Today, it has fallen to the individual to re-forge this link, by crafting new living myths that activate the archetypes as the old religions once did. With the traditional symbols serving as our guide and our raw material, we can build new myths out of the rubble. Such personal myths can serve as oases within our modern spiritual desert—islands of meaning amidst the contemporary barrenness. The individual is now the bearer of mythic meaning. As Campbell writes:

> And just as in the past each civilization was the vehicle of its own mythology, ... so in this modern world... each individual is

the center of a mythology of his own, of which his own intelligible character is the Incarnate God, so to say, whom his empirically questing consciousness is to find. The aphorism of Delphi, "Know thyself," is the motto. And not Rome, not Mecca, not Jerusalem, Sinai, or Benares, but each and every "thou" on earth is the center of this world...[1]

To date, the idea of personal myth has remained too modest. Campbell's "four functions of myth" provide a very useful schema for thinking about what a robust mythology truly accomplishes, personally and collectively. As we have seen, personal mythmaking, developed into a way of life, is able to fulfill *all* of the functions of myth, not just one or two. It is far more than just a form of therapy, or a way of thinking about the events of your life. Rather, it has the potential to transform the world, and render a service even to the Divine. It is the way to transform our horizons, the power by which we learn to tell a new story and gain a new aspiration for mankind.

Fortunately, we are not called to build this Cathedral all by ourselves, only to do our part. Every life is an addition, another canvas for a unique insight into consciousness. Every moment is an opportunity for the divine to develop. Every time you go your own way, another brick is laid. Every time you reach a deeper understanding of yourself, the Deity grows more awake. In the New Myth, stasis is the only sin; to grow, to learn, to live: *that* is your worship. God does not need another reciter of orthodoxy or Scripture-thumping conformist. God needs *individuals*, characters, weirdos. God needs *you—as you are*. So make a beginning. Your life is mythic. Live mythically.

In *A Religion of One's Own*, Thomas Moore reflects on one particular man's cathedral—Henry David Thoreau's. While visiting Walden Pond, Moore's mind wandered; he became lost in fantasy:

> I had a little daydream of Thoreau making the short journey from the town of Concord to the outpost of Walden and building his ten-by-fifteen-foot cabin in the spirit of the old cathedral builders. They were building a house for God, as was Thoreau in his more modest way. In the end, he wrote a small bible, *Walden*, a verbal companion to his tiny cathedral that contains a myriad of mundane details as a perfect background for profound insights into the spiritual life. You could do no better than to read his words again and again, placing them next to *Tao Te Ching* and the Gospel stories and some poems from Rumi and Hafiz. But the main task would be to emulate Thoreau and follow your own inspiration and build your own "cathedral," however personal and freely adapted, and create your own Bible and *Walden*.[2]

Our horizons tell our stories.
Help change them—by telling *yours*.

NOTES

SURVEYING

[1] Joseph Campbell (1968) *Creative Mythology* (Penguin, New York), 5; emphasis added.

[2] Carl Jung (1961) *Memories, Dreams, and Reflections* (Vintage Books, New York), 171; emphasis added.

[3] It should be noted that, to call *Memories, Dreams, Reflections* a "memoir" is not, strictly speaking, accurate, since large portions were largely ghost-written or otherwise heavily redacted by hands other than Jung's. Nevertheless, it still serves more or less as Jung's "authorized autobiography."

[4] Carl Jung (1956), *Symbols of Transformation* (Princeton University Press, Princeton, NJ), xxiv-xxv.

[5] *Memories, Dreams, Reflections*, 173.

[6] Ibid., 174.

[7] Ibid., 174.

[8] Ibid., 174.

[9] Ibid., 174.

[10] Ibid., 188.

[11] Ibid., 185.

[12] Ibid., 223.

[13] Ibid., 225.

[14] Ibid., 225.

[15] Stephen Larsen (1990) *The Mythic Imagination: The Quest for Meaning through Personal Mythology* (Inner Traditions, Rochester, VT), 15.

[16] *Creative Mythology*, 93; emphasis original.

[17] Dan P. McAdams (1993) *The Stories We Live By: Personal Myths and the Making of the Self* (The Guilford Press, New York), 34.

[18] David Feinstein, Stanley Krippner (2008) *Personal Mythology: Using Ritual, Dreams, and Imagination to Discover Your Inner Story* (Energy Psychology Press, Santa Rosa, CA), 6.

[19] Adapted from *Creative Mythology*, 4-6, 621-24; *Pathways to Bliss* (New World Library, Novato, CA), 105-107; and Lectures: "The Inward Journey," "The Thresholds of Mythology," "Oriental Mythology, "Confrontation of East and West in Religion," and "Mythology in the Modern Age."

DRAFTING

[1] Friedrich Nietzsche (1887) *The Gay Science* (trans. Walter Kaufmann) (Vintage, New York), 181.

[2] Leo Tolstoy, *Confessions*, quoted in William James, *The Varieties of Religious Experience* (Penguin, New York), 153.

[3] Jean-Paul Sartre, *Nausea*, 11.5.

[4] Dan McAdams, *The Stories We Live By*, 12.

[5] William James (1963) *Pragmatism and Other Essays* (Washington Square Press, New York), 208-209.

[6] D. Stephenson, Bond (1993) *Living Myth: Personal Meaning as a Way of Life* (Shambhala, Boston), 26.

[7] *Living Myth* 18-19.

[8] *Living Myth*, 19.

[9] Joseph Campbell (1959) *The Masks of God: Primitive Mythology* (Penguin, New York), 21-22, 28.

[10] Friedrich Nietzsche, *Human, All Too Human*, §292.

[11] Joseph Campbell, *Creative Mythology*, 6.

[12] From the Lecture "The Thresholds of Mythology."

THE BLUEPRINT

[1] Joseph Campbell, *Pathways to Bliss*, 88.

[2] Joseph Campbell (2001) *Thou Art That* (New World Library, Novato, CA), 24.

[3] *Pathways to Bliss*, 104-105.

[4] Campbell, Lecture: "The Thresholds of Mythology."

[5] Campbell, Lecture: "Mythology in the Modern Age."

[6] Joseph Campbell (1997) *The Mythic Dimension: Selected Essays 1959-1987* (New World Library, Novato, CA), 238.

[7] Edward Edinger (1992) *Ego and Archetype* (Shambhala, Boston), 101.

[8] Joseph Campbell (1986) *The Inner Reaches of Outer Space: Metaphor as Myth and as Religion* (New World Library, Novato, CA), 104.

[9] Rudolf Otto (1923) *The Idea of the Holy* (Oxford University Press, London), 12-13.

[10] Campbell, Lecture: "The Inward Journey."

[11] Bond, *Living Myth*, 51.

MATERIALS

[1] Sam Keen (1990) *To A Dancing God* (HarperCollins, New York), 99.

[2] Thomas Moore (2014) *A Religion of One's Own: A Guide to Creating a Personal Spirituality in a Secular World* (Gotham Books, New York), 4.

[3] Campbell, *Pathways to Bliss*, 97.

[4] *A Religion of One's Own*, 8.

[5] *A Religion of One's Own*, 28, 31.

[6] Campbell, *Creative Mythology*, 677-78.

[7] Daniele Bolelli (2013) *Create Your Own Religion: A How-To Book without Directions* (Disinformation Books, San Francisco), 33.

[8] Bond, *Living Myth*, 70-71.

[9] Larsen, *The Mythic Imagination*, 11.

[10] Campbell, *Creative Mythology*, 7.

CONSTRUCTION

[1] Campbell, *Creative Mythology*, 35-36.

[2] McAdams, *The Stories We Live By*, 122.

[3] Larsen, *Mythic Imagination*, 204.

[4] *The Stories We Live By*, 131.

[5] *The Stories We Live By*, 12.

[6] *Creative Mythology*, 40.

[7] Campbell, *Thou Art That*, 38-39.

[8] Leo Damrosch (2015) *Eternity's Sunrise: The Imaginative World of William Blake* (Yale University Press, New Haven, CT), 155.

[9] *Eternity's Sunrise*, 156.

[10] *Creative Mythology*, 614.

[11] *Creative Mythology*, 4.

[12] Bond, *Living Myth*, 138.

[13] *Living Myth*, 131.

[14] Campbell, *The Mythic Dimension*, 238.

[15] *Creative Mythology*, 92-93.

[16] *Creative Mythology*, 6.

MASTER PLAN

[1] McAdams, *The Stories We Live By*, 37.

[2] Bond, *Living Myth*, 29.

[3] *Living Myth*, 75.

[4] Alex and Allyson Grey, https://www.cosm.org/calendar/art-church.

[5] Alex Grey (1998) *The Mission of Art* (Shambala, Boulder), 150.

[6] *The Mission of Art*, 24.

[7] *Living Myth*, 76.

[8] Edward F. Edinger (1984) *The Creation of Consciousness: Jung's Myth for Modern Man* (Inner City Books, Toronto), 11.

[9] Bond, *Living Myth*, 191.

[10] Jung, *Memories, Dreams, Reflections*, 251-252.

[11] Ibid., 252.

[12] Ibid., 255-256.

[13] Ibid., 339.

[14] Ibid., 338.

[15] *The Creation of Consciousness*, 56.

[16] *The Creation of Consciousness*, 31.

[17] James, *The Varieties of Religious Experience*, 392-393.

[18] *The Creation of Consciousness*, 113.

[19] Edward F. Edinger (1996) *The New God-Image: A Study of Jung's Key Letters concerning the Evolution of the Western God-Image* (Chiron Publications, Ashville, NC), 113.

[20] *Living Myth*, 191.

[21] Campbell, *Creative Mythology*, p. 5; emphasis added.

[22] *Pathways to Bliss*, 91.

[23] *The Creation of Consciousness*, 25-27.

[24] *The Creation of Consciousness*, 25-27.

[25] *The Creation of Consciousness*, 27.

EPILOGUE: GETTING TO WORK

[1] Campbell, *Creative Mythology*, 36.

[2] Moore, *A Religion of One's Own*, 9.

Made in the USA
Monee, IL
10 May 2024

58300008R00069